Dickens
of London

and Now stir the fire and close the shutters fast
let fall the curtains wheel round
the sofa and the bubbling loud
hissing Urn throws up a steamy
column + the cups that cheer
But not inebriate wait on
each other so let us welcome
peaceful evening in

William

Christmas
1980.

#6a

Wolf Mankowitz

Dickens
of London

Weidenfeld and Nicolson
LONDON

Designed by Craig Dodd
for George Weidenfeld and Nicolson Ltd
11 St John's Hill, London SW11

ISBN 0 297 77159 0

Printed in Great Britain by
Butler & Tanner Ltd,
Frome and London

Contents

Contents continued

Chapter One

No Distance
and No Time

CHARLES DICKENS WAS BORN IN LANDPORT, A DISTRICT OF Portsmouth, on 7 February 1812. In Spain, the Duke of Wellington that year defeated the French at Badajoz and Salamanca; Napoleon turned eastwards, and disastrously marched towards Moscow. England was also conducting a futile war with America, thirty-six years after the Declaration of Independence. Although both engagements impinged upon the work of Charles's father, John Dickens, a clerk in the Navy Pay Office, there were events nearer home which would prove more significant to the grown novelist than the Government's foreign affairs. The first passenger steamboat service was launched on the Clyde, George Stephenson was building a steam locomotive that travelled at six miles an hour – the Industrial Revolution was starting to transform the country. But the urban concentration, unemployment and starving poverty that it would accelerate were held off, in 1812, only by the Government's levies of men and supplies for the wars abroad. Within four years there would be a Corn Law to keep up the price of food, and rioting in London and the countryside.

Right: Portsmouth, Dickens's birthplace and home town from 1812–14

8

In Charles Dickens's own home life there occurred, too, an apparently minor event, when he was only four months old, that signalled what would be the formative experiences of his life. John Dickens could no longer afford the rent of the modest terraced house, although it cost only a quarter of his £140 annual salary, and the family moved into a smaller, cramped home. Still, the naval town, with its bustling dockyard, ferry-rides to Gosport, sailors and soldiers on parade and the stagecoach jingling in from London, was a lively enough place for a little boy, with his sister Fanny, a year older, and a maid to look after them.

John Dickens was the son of servants to the noble Crewe family. His father had died when John was still a baby, but Lord Crewe had interested himself in the Dickens children, and used his influence to obtain the naval clerical post for John. That was a step up for the young man; but, perhaps in emulation of the grand life he had seen from below stairs, John Dickens always took more steps at a time than he could manage within his means. He loved to entertain his friends with good drink and conversation, discoursing with an inventive, elaborate humour. A conscientious husband, father and clerk, he had no vice in him, just a weakness for the grand gesture too often, and he never overcame it. Throughout his life he was short of money and reduced to humble expedients, borrowing to pay debts that he would repay with more borrowing.

It was through his work in the Navy Pay Office that John had met Elizabeth Barrow, a pretty, amusing and educated girl whom he married when she was

Below: Dickens's parents, John and Elizabeth Dickens

eighteen and he twenty-three. She was the sister of one of John Dickens's fellow clerks; her father, Charles Barrow, was also employed by the Navy Pay Office in London, in the very senior rank of Chief Conductor of Moneys in Town. Shortly after the marriage Charles Barrow was accused of embezzlement; in seven years he had mulcted the Navy Board of over £5000. He confessed, and fled the country for ever. John Dickens may have felt some sympathy for his father-in-law, who had ten children to support and much illness in the family; but it was a lash of ill fortune to a man who must certainly have been looking to his wife's well-connected family to assist his own.

Elizabeth herself was not obviously prudent, either. A few hours before Charles was born, his mother had accepted an invitation to a ball. She danced into the small hours, returned home, and before dawn bore the son christened Charles John Huffam Dickens.

In 1814 John Dickens was transferred back to Somerset House, in London, where he had worked previously. The family, increased by the birth of Letitia in 1816, stayed in London for three years, of which Charles later remembered little. In the middle of 1817, however, John Dickens was transferred again, to work in the naval dockyard at Chatham, and it was there, in the Medway Valley, that the novelist's earliest and happiest clear memories were formed.

John Dickens's salary had risen, and so, in geometrical proportions, had his pretensions. He rented 2 Ordnance Terrace, a three-storey house close to the Kentish countryside, with views across Chatham and the valley. He engaged two servants, one of whom, Mary Weller, took care of the three children. Also living in the household was Elizabeth's widowed sister, Aunt Fanny.

Mary Weller had a ghoulish way of arousing Charles Dickens's imagination, if ever that prodigious force needed arousing at any age. A standard bedtime story would dwell on one Captain Murderer, whose taste in wives was literally indulged when they were baked in pies. His own fate was more severe still, and related in detail. Another evil character suffered torture by rats. All these events, Mary Weller told him, had happened to people she knew quite well. Charles, on his own admission later in life, was left lying in bed rigid with terror. Other bedtimes were calmer, the capricious Mary humming the evening hymn, while Charles wept 'either with the remorseful consciousness of having kicked Somebody else, or because still Somebody else had hurt my feelings'. Even by day, a child then was exposed to sights that few in England would witness now: a monstrous childbirth, five at a time, the little dead bodies laid out 'side by side, on a clean cloth on a chest of drawers', like 'pigs' feet as they are usually displayed at a neat tripe-shop'.

But there were healthier joys. In the fields around the house Charles grew stronger and merrier than he had been in London, where according to his friend

and biographer, John Forster, he had been 'a very little and a very sickly boy....
He was never a good little cricket player, he was never a first-rate hand at marbles
or peg-top, or prisoners' base; but he had great pleasure in watching the other
boys, officers' sons for the most part, at these games, reading while they played.'
He was 'a terrible boy to read', Mary Weller said. His mother had taught him
the alphabet. 'What fat black letters to begin with!' Dickens later remembered.

'A was an archer, who shot at a frog.' Of course he was. He was an apple-pie also,
and there he is! He was a good many things in his time, was A. And so were most of
his friends, except X, who had so little versatility that I never knew him to get beyond
Xerxes or Xantippe – like Y, who was always confined to a Yacht or a Yew Tree; and
Z condemned for ever to be a Zebra or a Zany.

He was already reading avidly when, with his sister Fanny, he was sent to a school
run by a dame with a hard knuckle for small heads.

Next door to the Dickens house lived Lucy Stroughill, 'a peach-faced creature
in a blue sash', who sat with him under the table at her birthday party eating
cakes. With Lucy and her brother the Dickens children spent days in games and
plays, magic-lantern shows and comic duets. Charles's talent for dramatic recitations and duets with Fanny was one that his father loved to show off to friends
and visitors.

John Dickens, with an increased salary now, saw himself as a substantial citizen.
He contributed to charitable causes in the town, and was not to be confined in
his expansive gestures by the birth of two more children, Harriet and Frederick.
By 1821, however, he could no longer afford to pay the rent of their pleasant house,

*Below: Chatham in the
Medway valley where
Dickens spent the five
happiest years of his
childhood from 1817–22*

and the family moved again, down into the streets of Chatham. Charles was not put out by the move, for it allowed him opportunities to walk around the town with his father, taking in the sights and sounds and smells of the busy dockyard: the shipwrights, the anchorsmiths, convict labourers ('with great numbers on their backs as if they were street doors'), the rope, wood and canvas, grand buildings and pageants. There was the London coach office, and the Guild Hall which seemed so 'glorious' that it might have been 'the model on which the Genie of the Lamp built the palace for Aladdin'. There was the cathedral and the old, ruined castle on the hill, and Chatham Lines, where the regiments paraded, as they had done in Portsmouth. With his father, he could go sailing on the Medway or take long country walks. One such walk brought them to Gad's Hill, the site of a scene as comic as any Shakespeare wrote – Falstaff's robbery. There stood an elegant house called Gad's Hill Place, which moved John Dickens to preach

Right: Mr Grimaldi, the great nineteenth-century clown whom Dickens saw and loved as a child, and whose memoirs he was later to edit

M.ʳ GRIMALDI, as Clown.

12

a sermon to his son that, by dint of very hard work and extraordinary success, he might one day inhabit that house. It was a paternal sermon that, for once, came true.

Stimulated by these outward scenes, the boy was no less stirred in his imagination by his father's cheap editions of novels that he found

> ... in a little room upstairs to which I had access (for it adjoined my own), and which nobody else in our house ever troubled. From that blessed little room, *Roderick Random*, *Peregrine Pickle*, *Humphrey Clinker*, *Tom Jones*, *The Vicar of Wakefield*, *Don Quixote*, *Gil Blas*, and *Robinson Crusoe* came out, a glorious host, to keep me company.... I have been Tom Jones (a child's Tom Jones, a harmless creature) for a week together. I have sustained my own idea of Roderick Random for a month at a stretch, I verily believe. I had a greedy relish for a few volumes of Voyages and Travels – I forget what, now – that were on those shelves; and for days and days I can remember to have gone about my region of our house, armed with the centrepiece out of an old set of boot-trees – the perfect realization of Captain Somebody, of the Royal British Navy, in danger of being beset by savages, and resolved to sell his life at a great price....
>
> When I think of it, the picture always arises in my mind of a summer evening, the boys at play in the churchyard, and I sitting on my bed, reading as if for life.

And as well as books, there was the theatre, a profession that was very nearly to claim him, and with which he was always more than half in love. He had seen pantomimes in London – the real old pantomimes, with Harlequin and Columbine, and Pantaloon – and once he saw the great clown Grimaldi, whose memoirs he was to edit later. In Chatham and Rochester he now saw not only pantomime but farces and melodramas. He was taken to them by Dr Matthew Lamert, an army surgeon who was courting Charles's widowed Aunt Fanny.

Lamert's son by a former marriage, James, was keen on amateur theatricals, and the boy watched their rehearsals with such enthusiasm that shortly he himself composed a short tragedy entitled *Misnor, the Sultan of India*. When Dr Lamert and Aunt Fanny married and moved to Ireland, James stayed in Chatham, lodging with the Dickens family, and interested himself in Charles, taking him to see *Richard III*, *Macbeth*, and lesser dramas.

Another educated young man who recognized Charles's promise was William Giles, son of a long-winded preacher whose mannerisms – 'looking up the inside of his outstretched coat-sleeve as if it were a telescope with the stopper on' – permanently disenchanted Charles with nonconformism. The younger Giles, however, was a much brighter character than his father, and at the school he ran, which Charles and Fanny attended for some eighteen months, the ten-year-old boy quickly and happily advanced in his studies. He enjoyed the friendships he made there, too, and the boisterous games, the rowing on the Medway and skating on frozen ponds, the Guy Fawkes bonfires and Twelfth-Night parties.

In late 1822, the happy and growing days in Chatham were ended by the transfer

13

of John Dickens back to the London office. The loss of childhood is a bruise in anyone's life. To Charles, aged nearly eleven, the contrast between his childhood in Chatham and what now awaited him in London was a wound so severe that he never let it heal.

Probably he stayed behind a few weeks in Chatham to finish his school term with Mr Giles, while the rest of the family moved to London. If so, a passage in *David Copperfield* can be read as the novelist's memory of bidding his family goodbye:

> I think as Mrs Micawber sat at the back of the coach with the children, and I stood in the road looking wistfully at them, a mist cleared from her eyes, and she saw what a little creature I really was. I think so, because she beckoned me to climb up, with quite a new and motherly expression in her face, and put her arms around my neck, and gave me just such a kiss as she might have given to her own boy.

Charles himself left Chatham by coach on a grey, damp morning, and would never forget 'the smell of the damp straw in which I was packed – like game – and forwarded carriage-paid, to the Cross Keys, Wood Street, Cheapside. There was no other inside passenger, and I consumed my sandwiches in solitude and dreariness, and it rained hard all the way, and I thought that life was sloppier than I had expected to find it.'

Right: A note from the twelve-year-old Dickens to a schoolfriend

Chapter Two

Cast Away

BEFORE LEAVING CHATHAM, THE DICKENS FAMILY HAD SOLD off household goods to pay some of the debts incurred by John Dickens's improvidence. Now, in Camden Town, they crammed themselves into a house with four rooms, basement and garret – the parents, six children (including a new baby, Alfred), a maid-of-all-work, and James Lamert. These economies were not enough to satisfy the creditors, and Charles heard his parents speaking in low voices about 'The Deed'. He imagined some frightful deed that his father had

Right: The small house in Bayham Street, Camden Town, to which the ten-strong Dickens household moved late in 1822

committed, and for which retribution was impending. The Deed was in fact a composition of his debts that John Dickens had agreed with the creditors; after which tidying-up, he seems to have felt that little more could be expected of him. If there were insistent demands, something would turn up, or the better-off relatives would help him through.

One further economy he did make, however, and it pierced Charles to the heart. He described it, later in his life, to John Forster:

As I thought in the little back garret in Bayham Street, of all I had lost in losing Chatham, what would I have given, if I had had anything to give, to have been sent back to any other school, to have been taught something anywhere!

I know my father to be as kind-hearted and generous a man as ever lived in the world. Everything that I can remember of his conduct to his wife, or children, or friends, in sickness or affliction, is beyond all praise. By me, as a sick child, he has watched night and day, unweariedly and patiently, many nights and days. He never undertook any business, charge or trust, that he did not zealously, conscientiously, punctually, honourably discharge. His industry has always been untiring. He was proud of me, in his way, and had a great admiration of the comic singing. But, in the ease of his temper, and the straitness of his means, he appeared to have utterly lost at this time the idea of educating me at all, and to have utterly put from him the notion that I had any claim upon him, in that regard, whatever. So I degenerated into cleaning his boots of a morning, and my own; and making myself useful in the work of that little house; and looking after my younger brothers and sisters; and going on such poor errands as arose out of our poor way of living.

Salting the wound was a scholarship that his older sister Fanny had won to the Royal Academy of Music, where she went as a boarder. He missed her companionship very much, and at the same time could only, helplessly, envy the opportunity she had to advance her education, while he, without friends nearby, spent his idle time wandering around Camden Town, and gazing across the wasteland that lay before London, where the dome of St Paul's loomed through the smoke, arousing in him 'hours of vague reflection afterwards'.

Gradually he started to wander further afield. The ramshackle houses and shops of Camden Town, the small factories, taverns and eating-houses, rubbish dumps and frowzy fields, no longer sufficiently fed the inner, imaginative world into which he was escaping from neglect at home. He would walk down through Holborn and into the City. Once, reading a humorous book at home, he was galvanized by a description of Covent Garden into running down there at once, to breathe in 'the flavour of the faded cabbage-leaves as if it were the very breath of comic fiction' – that alchemy of real things into story of which he was destined to be the great wizard, and which he was already beginning to practise in character-sketches of his own. Another time he got lost in the Strand with a shilling and fourpence in his pocket, given to him by his godfather. He started to cry, like

Right: Too poor to go to school, Dickens used to wander through the crowded, noisy slums of London. In this view of Tyndall's Buildings Gray's Inn Lane, a pauper's coffin is carried unnoticed through the crowd

any child, then felt hungry and walked along looking in the windows of food shops, mustering the courage to go in and buy something.

At last I saw a pile of cooked sausages in a window with the label, 'Small Germans, a Penny'. Emboldened by knowing what to ask for, I went in and said, 'if you please, will you sell me a small German?' which they did.... Thus I wandered about the City, like a child in a dream, staring at the British merchants, and inspired by a mighty faith in the marvellousness of everything. Up courts and down courts – in and out of yards and little squares – peeping into counting-house passages and running away.

He was chased off by cooks he stared at, and, being respectably dressed, was quite savagely menaced by a gang of boys he met. He went into a theatre, where the conversation around him in the gallery 'was not improving'. When he came out it was dark and raining, and he felt 'unspeakably forlorn', and worried about the anxiety his family would be feeling. A watchman with a dreadful cough helped him back to his parents. 'They used to say I was an odd child, and I suppose I was.'

He was taken into London sometimes to see relatives, and was bewitched by

18

what he saw, especially returning at night: streets thronged with hurrying crowds and noisy vehicles, muffin-boys, chimney-sweeps, apprentices, gin-parlours and cooked-food stalls, the gaslamps and the darknesses between them, and the sinister district of Seven Dials – 'what wild visions of prodigies of wickedness, want, and beggary arose in my mind out of that place!' The coach rattled home through paradoxes later described in *Nicholas Nickleby*:

The rags of the squalid ballad-singer fluttered in the rich light that showed the gold-smith's treasures, pale and pinched-up faces hovered about the windows where was tempting food, hungry eyes wandered over the profusion guarded by one thin sheet of brittle glass – an iron wall to them; half-naked shivering figures stopped to gaze at Chinese shawls and golden stuffs of India.

There were trips to Limehouse where his godfather Christopher Huffam, a rigger, lived 'in a substantial handsome sort of way'. The ramshackle, decaying water-front of the Thames, river of trades and suicides, filled his memory with images that surfaced in the books he was to write. His own reading at this time was encouraged by being lent *The Spectator* and *The Tatler*, Holbein's *Dance of Death*, George Colman's *Broad Grins*, by a bookseller's widow who lived below the Gerrard Street, Soho, lodgings of his uncle, Thomas Barrow.

But at home, in Camden Town, the beloved books of his Chatham days were sold, one by one, to pay debts. Charles himself had the painful job of taking *Tom Jones, Peregrine Pickle* and the rest to a drunken bookseller. (He promised himself that one day he would replace every volume, and he did.) A few shillings for books and other goods would not go far, however, so Elizabeth Dickens decided that she must take an initiative in her husband's tangled affairs. She paid the rent, more than twice what they paid in Camden Town, on an impressive building in Gower Street, affixed a brass plate that read MRS DICKENS'S ESTABLISHMENT, and waited for pupils to troop in. 'Nobody ever came to the school', Dickens remembered, 'nor do I recollect that anybody ever proposed to come, or that the least preparation was made to receive anybody.'

Meanwhile, angry tradesmen continued to dun John Dickens, as a passage in *David Copperfield* plainly recalls. Creditors

...used to come at all hours, and some of them were quite ferocious. One dirty-faced man, I think he was a bootmaker, used to edge himself into the passage as early as seven o'clock in the morning, and call up the stairs to Mr Micawber – 'Come! You ain't out yet, you know. Pay us, will you? Don't hide, you know; that's mean. I wouldn't be mean if I was you. Pay us, will you! You just pay us, d'ye hear? Come!' Receiving no answer to these taunts, he would mount in his wrath to the words 'swindlers' and 'robbers'; and these being ineffectual too, would sometimes go to the extremity of cross-ing the street, and roaring up at the windows of the second floor, where he knew Mr Micawber was. At these times Mr Micawber would be transported with grief and mor-tification, even to the length as I was once made aware by a scream from his wife, of making motions at himself with a razor; but within half an hour afterwards, he would polish up his shoes with extraordinary pains, and go out, humming a tune with a greater air of gentility than ever. Mrs Micawber was quite as elastic.

Charles himself was not as elastic. The kidney spasms that, in his infancy, had attacked the 'sickly boy' were now brought on again. Throughout his life, he was subject to the same trouble at times of stress or fatigue.

James Lamert saw how badly things were going for the Dickens family and came up with a proposition. Charles had little enough to do, beyond small errands: why did he not go out to work at the boot-blacking factory of which Lamert, now lodging elsewhere, had lately become the manager? During the dinner-hour, Lamert added kindly, he would undertake to give the boy some school lessons every day. Mr and Mrs Dickens at once accepted the offer, and the following Monday morning, two days after his twelfth birthday, Charles reported to the factory at Hungerford Stairs, on the river below the Strand. The hours, 8 am to 8 pm, and the wage, six shillings a week, were both quite reasonable for that time, and there was nothing at all unusual in a boy working at the age of twelve: many started four or five years earlier. The job, at which Charles had no difficulty in excelling, was to paper and label the pots of blacking. At first he was given a privileged position, overlooking the river, in which to do his work; but soon

Below left: Limehouse–a ramshackle, decaying waterfront of the Thames where Dickens went to visit his godfather, Christopher Huffam
Below right: The blacking factory (left) at Hungerford Stairs, where the twelve-year-old Dickens miserably worked – labelling the pots of blacking

he was moved downstairs into the common workroom of the rat-run, tumbledown building, where the other lads mockingly referred to him as 'the young gentleman', and Lamert's lunchtime lessons ceased.

This sudden and unlooked-for turn in his life shocked Charles's idea of himself so profoundly that he kept the episode secret, even from his children, until he died; but it preyed so constantly on his mind that he hinted at it time and again in his books and talk. In a fragment of autobiography that he never published, he wrote:

It is wonderful to me how I could have been so easily cast away at such an age. It is wonderful to me, that, even after my descent into the poor little drudge I had been since we came to London, no one had compassion enough on me – a child of singular abilities, quick, eager, delicate, and soon hurt, bodily or mentally – to suggest that something might have been spared, as certainly it might have been, to place me at any common school. Our friends, I take it, were tired out. No one made any sign, my father and mother were quite satisfied. They could hardly have been more so, if I had been twenty years of age, distinguished at a grammar-school, and going to Cambridge....

No words can express the secret agony of my soul, as I sunk into this companionship; compared these everyday associates with those of my happier childhood; and felt my early hopes of growing up to be a learned and distinguished man, crushed in my breast.

The deep remembrance of the sense I had of being utterly neglected and hopeless; of the shame I felt in my position; of the misery it was to my young heart to believe that, day by day, what I had learned, and thought, and delighted in, and raised my fancy and my emulation up by, was passing away from me, never to be brought back any more; cannot be written. My whole nature was so penetrated with the grief and humiliation of such considerations, that even now, famous and caressed and happy, I often forget in my dreams that I have a dear wife and children; even that I am a man; and wander desolately back to that time of my life.... I never said, to man or boy, how it was that I came to be there, or gave the least indication of being sorry that I was there. That I suffered in secret, and that I suffered exquisitely, no one ever knew but I.

He had been working at the blacking factory less than two weeks when his father was arrested for debt. After a weekend in which the tearful family sent Charles on vain errands to raise the cash immediately wanted, John Dickens was committed to the Marshalsea debtors' prison in Southwark. As he entered the gate, he wept to Charles that the sun had set upon him for ever, words that Charles 'really believed had broken my heart'. In prison, he remained at first a tragic figure, though still orotund in utterance, admonishing his son, who visited him in the evenings, to take heed of his wretched example.

Afterwards, Charles would walk home to Gower Street and be sent out, with a few more items from the household's dwindling stock, to the pawnshop. There the clerk would hear him conjugate a Latin verb while the ticket was written out. 'My own little bed', Dickens wrote, 'was so superciliously looked upon by a power unknown to me, hazily called "The Trade", that a brass coal-scuttle, a toasting-jack, and a bird-cage were obliged to be put with it to make a Lot of it, and then it went for a song – so I heard mentioned, and I wondered what song – and thought what a dismal song it must be to sing.' In feeding the family, everything finally went to the pawnshop save a few chairs and beds, and the kitchen table. After that, there was nothing to do but relinquish Gower Street and move into the Marshalsea with John Dickens.

It was a common procedure for all the family to live together in the debtor's cell. John Dickens's naval salary was still being paid to him, and the rest of the family were allowed to roam in and out of the prison by day. Even the maid continued to visit them every morning and wait upon them. John Dickens's spirits began to rise again, and he became chairman of the prisoners' social arrangements.

Charles, however, did not live in the Marshalsea, but back in Camden Town in lodgings his father paid for. His food and everything else had to be supplied from the six shillings a week he earned. A sausage and a penny loaf with a little milk, or bread and cheese and a glass of beer, or a fourpenny plate of beef and some coffee, these were his staple dishes. Sometimes he could not resist spending what should have been his dinner money on a pastry, a slice of bread-pudding, or a twopenny magazine. Once he entered a fine dining-house in Drury Lane, carrying his own bread and magnificently ordering a small plate of *à la mode* beef to eat with it. 'What the waiter thought of such a strange little apparition, coming in all alone, I don't know; but I can see him now, staring at me as I ate my dinner, and bringing up the other waiter to look. I gave him a halfpenny, and I wish, now, that he hadn't taken it.' On Saturday nights, with six shillings in his pocket, he afforded himself a treat. There was an evening when he went into the Red Lion in Parliament Street.

'What is your very best – the VERY *best* – ale, a glass?' For the occasion was a festive one, for some reason: I forget why. 'Twopence', says he. 'Then', says I, 'just draw me a glass of that if you please, with a good head to it.' The landlord looked at me, in return, over the bar, from head to foot, with a strange smile on his face; and instead of drawing the beer, looked round the screen and said something to his wife, who came out from behind it, with her work in her hand and joined in surveying me. . . . They asked me a good many questions, as to what my name was, how old I was, where I lived, how I was employed, etc., etc. To all of which, that I might commit nobody, I invented appropriate answers. They served me with the ale, though I suspect it was not the strongest on the premises; and the landlord's wife, opening the little half-door and bending down, gave me a kiss that was half-admiring and half-compassionate, but all womanly and good, I am sure.

When he had no money for food, in spite of wrapping up his wages in equal packages and labelling them with the days of the week, he would go to Covent Garden or the poultry-markets, and just stare. 'I know that, but for the mercy of God, I might easily have been, for any care that was taken of me, a little robber or a little vagabond.' His plight was dramatized when he watched his sister Fanny receive a prize at the Academy. 'The tears ran down my face. I prayed, when I went to bed that night, to be lifted out of the humiliation and neglect in which I was. I had never suffered so much before.'

It was with Fanny, one Sunday evening at the end of a day visiting the Marshalsea, that Charles broke down and wept to his father how lonely his life was. John

Left: An illustration by Phiz recalling the young Dickens's adventure in the Red Lion in Parliament Street

23

Dickens accordingly found him a pleasant attic room near the prison, and Charles was able to eat breakfast and supper with his family every day. But misery continued to aggravate his kidney spasms. One of them laid him low all day at work; a friend looked after him well and insisted on accompanying him home that evening, but Charles, too proud to let it be known where his family was living, had to enact a deceit to get rid of his companion before they arrived at the Marshalsea gate.

All the time, the details of the despondent streets of London, and of prison life, were imprinting themselves on his memory, whence they would one day issue, with no loss of observed detail, into the books he wrote. The image and metaphor of prison, too, took hold on his imagination permanently.

After three months in the Marshalsea, something turned up for John Dickens. His mother died, leaving him £450, enough to discharge him from the prison. The family moved back to Camden Town, John Dickens resumed his job, and Charles waited for release from his own prison of despair in the blacking factory, which had now moved to premises on Bedford Street. But he never 'heard a word of being taken away, or of being otherwise than quite provided for', and was 'just as solitary and self-dependent as before'. In the new place, Charles worked in the street window, where anyone passing could watch him. 'I saw my father coming in at the door one day when we were very busy, and I wondered how he could bear it.'

Shortly afterwards, John Dickens gave his son a note to carry to James Lamert. Whatever the contents, it provoked a fierce quarrel between the two men about Charles, with the result that Lamert said that he was much insulted and Charles could not work for him any longer. 'I cried very much, partly because it was so sudden, and partly because in his anger he was violent about my father, though gentle to me ... with a relief so strange that it was like oppression, I went home.' Home to a mother who set out to repair the quarrel, and succeeded, so that Charles was invited to resume his job the next morning. No, said John Dickens, the boy should go to school again. Charles never forgave his mother, 'never afterwards forgot, I never shall forget, I never can forget, that my mother was warm for my being sent back'.

His time in the blacking factory had spanned perhaps twenty weeks, but for all he had known it might have endured twenty years. He never walked near the place, and encountering his old route home to Gower Street made the grown man cry. The delicate, small boy with long curls had, in a sense, died, as Edgar Johnson remarks in his indispensable biography, 'to be succeeded by a man of deadly determination, of insuperable resolve, hard and aggressive almost to fierceness. In another, that child never died, but was continually reborn in a host of children suffering or dying young and other innocent victims undergoing injustice and pain.'

Chapter Three

A Great Splash

FOR NEARLY THREE YEARS CHARLES ATTENDED THE WELLINGTON House Academy in Hampstead Road. He was taught English, French, Latin, writing, mathematics, and dancing the hornpipe. With the other boys he kept birds and mice in cages, staged plays in a toy theatre, read penny dreadfuls, wrote stories and jokes for the school magazine, and was full of high spirits and japes.

In *The Uncommercial Traveller* he tells an anecdote concerning the change that came over the school bully, Globson, after Charles had received a letter with hints of treats to be sent him from the West Indies:

I had mentioned these hints in confidence to a few friends, and had promised to give away, as I now see reason to believe, a handsome covey of partridges potted, and about a hundredweight of guava jelly. It was now that Globson, bully no more, sought me out in the playground. He was a big fat boy, with a big fat head and a big fat fist, and at the beginning of that Half had raised such a bump on my forehead that I couldn't get my hat of state on, to go to Church. He said that after an interval of reflection (four months) he now felt this blow to have been an error of judgement, and that he wished to apologize for the same.

Not only that but holding down his big head between his two big hands in order that I might reach it conveniently, he requested me, as an act of justice which would appease his awakened conscience, to raise a retributive bump upon it, in the presence of witnesses.

This handsome proposal I modestly declined, and he then embraced me, and we walked away conversing. We conversed respecting the West India Islands, and, in the pursuit of knowledge, he asked me with much interest whether in the course of my reading I had met with any reliable description of the mode of manufacturing guava jelly; or whether I had ever happened to taste that conserve, which he had been given to understand was of rare excellence.

Outwardly Charles was a rather small, curly-haired, cheerful boy, who held his head proudly. No one at the school saw the rags in his heart. David Copperfield would ask: 'How could it affect them, who were so innocent of London life and London streets, to discover how knowing I was (and ashamed to be) in the meanest phases of both?'

By the spring of 1827 John Dickens had been dismissed from the Navy Pay Office after his dishonour in the Marshalsea. He had a small pension from the job, however, and he supplemented it by training his love of language into an aptitude for newspaper reporting. He secured a new job for himself as one of the parliamentary reporters for the *British Press*. Yet he was again hard pressed for cash. Another baby, Augustus, had been born, the rent could not be paid, and the Dickens family were evicted from their house, becoming lodgers in Somers Town. Charles's school fees were beyond them. This time his mother tapped family connections to get her son a position as office boy to an attorney's firm.

One May morning Charles reported for duty in the offices of Ellis and Blackmore, in Gray's Inn, his schoolboy spirits still cocky enough to fetch him a black eye or two. He would lean out of the second-floor window and drop cherry-stones on to passing hats, feigning such innocence when the wearers walked up to complain that they usually went off shaking their heads. But the job itself was boring and its ultimate prospects, the top of the law profession, did not attract him when he saw those who had spent a lifetime in it, splitting hairs slowly and growing rich on the distress of others – 'a very pleasant, profitable affair of private theatricals, presented to an uncommonly select audience'. With private amusement, he took note of the foibles and mannerisms of the people he met in the legal labyrinths: observations that not only served him later on in the characterizations of his novels, but also, for the present, whetted the alternative project he imagined for himself, journalism.

Through his father, he had, while still at school, earned an occasional shilling by reporting small local items for the *British Press*. Now, as his father had recently done, he applied himself to learning shorthand. After eighteen months at it, he had the confidence to leave Ellis and Blackmore and set himself up as a freelance reporter in Doctors' Commons, a muddle of law-courts near St Paul's where, sharing a rented box with a family connection who already knew the job, he sat waiting to be engaged to take down the court record of a case.

Soon the processes of law, seen from this new angle, became again too tedious to bear; and besides, so obscure and modestly rewarded a job did nothing for him in the bright eyes of Maria Beadnell, a banker's daughter whose eyes were now very important to him. He resolved to be an actor.

It was not a reckless decision. As a child his talent for comic songs and recitations had stood out, and recently he had been performing to a more critical audience at musical evenings that his sister Fanny, successfully graduated from the Royal Academy of Music, arranged with her friends. He had also developed a remarkable gift of mimicry. Walking London from end to end, at all hours of the clock, his observation of the characters he met was acute; he captured them in written sketches (many later worked into novels), and he recaptured them, to entertain his friends, by impersonating them. As well as the characters of street life, he was admired for his imitations of leading actors and singers of the time. Most evenings he visited a theatre, usually entering after nine o'clock, when the tickets were cheaper. His customary companion was a fellow clerk, Thomas Potter. Sharp dressers, they went out in the town for chops and oysters, stout or brandy-and-water, with cigars, and on to watch a play, a melodrama or variety show. Probably they sometimes acted in one of the 'private' theatres where, on payment of a fee, amateurs could play, say, the part of Richard III (£2), Buckingham (15s), Stanley (5s), or whatever took their fantasy.

Charles rehearsed thoroughly for his entrance to the profession. He took lessons in the actor's craft, and at home practised walking, sitting, gesture and voice. He modelled himself especially on an actor whom he could have seen at Chatham, and now certainly saw often in London: Charles Mathews, who was not simply a popular comic actor but also a singer, conjuror, and impersonator of such variety that he excelled in solo performances of a complete short play, taking every part. When Charles was ready, he wrote to the Lyceum Theatre for an audition and an appointment was made. With Fanny to accompany him, he was 'to do anything of Mathews's I pleased, before him and Charles Kemble'. On the appointed day, he was 'laid up with a terrible bad cold' and had to postpone his audition.

During the same period, he did not spend all his leisure time gadding about. On his eighteenth birthday, the youngest permissible age, he had obtained a reader's ticket at the British Museum, and there in the Reading Room spent days that he was to account 'the usefullest of my life', advancing his education.

The postponed audition never took place. At the age of twenty he was offered the chance of becoming a journalist, the project for which he had sweated to learn shorthand and started to despair of in the tedium of court records. His mother's brother, John Henry Barrow, a *Times* reporter, had initiated *The Mirror of Parliament*, a rival of *Hansard*. John Dickens was already one of its reporters; now Charles was invited to join, and he gladly accepted. At the same time, he was also invited to join the general reporting staff of a new evening paper, the *True Sun*, which he did from its first day of publication.

Within a short time in the gallery at Westminster, where no provision for reporters was made by an unaccommodating Parliament, he 'made a great splash', as he put it. Among his colleagues, to whom he was courteous but exceedingly reserved, others concurred: he 'occupied the very highest rank, not merely for accuracy in reporting, but for marvellous quickness in transcript', one of them attested. 'There never *was* such a shorthand writer', another declared. Further testimony comes from Edward Stanley, the Chief Secretary, who had spoken in the House on the Irish question – a debate in which Daniel O'Connell, describing the sufferings of the Irish, had so moved Charles that he put down his pencil, hid his face, and wept. The length of Stanley's speech was such that Charles, having reported the first forty-five minutes, was recalled to report the end too, seven other reporters having served their stint meanwhile. When the report of his speech was published Stanley, wishing it to be circulated·in Ireland, was disturbed by the inaccuracy he found in all the report save the beginning and end of it, and asked Barrow to send him the reporter who was responsible for those parts. He wanted to dictate the whole speech to him. Charles was brought back from a restful Sunday in the country, and ushered into Stanley's office in Carlton House Terrace. Stanley entered, eyed him, and said 'I beg pardon, but I had hoped to see the gentleman who had reported part of my speech.' 'I am that gentleman', Charles answered. 'Oh, indeed', Stanley said, amused. Striding up and

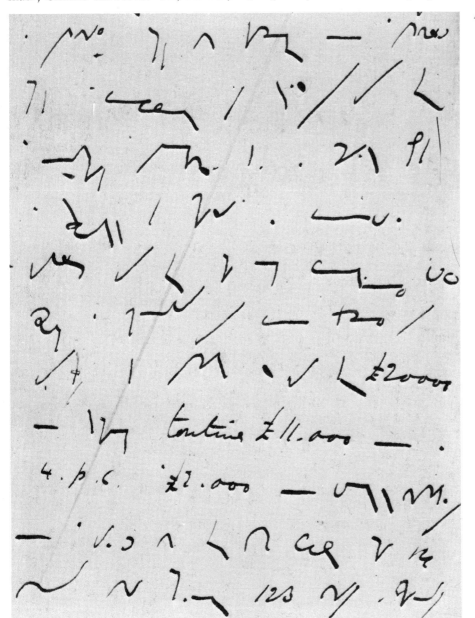

Left: A page of Dickens's shorthand notes

Overleaf: The House of Commons, in 1833

down, Stanley now repeated his speech, 'hour after hour, to the end, often becoming very much excited, and frequently bringing down his hand with great violence upon the desk'. Afterwards, Stanley wrote to Barrow complimenting him upon a reporter so able, and so youthful.

The Parliament that Dickens watched at work was, by its own standards, a distinguished one, including Lord Grey, Lord John Russell, Gladstone, Macaulay, Cobbett, and O'Connell. It abolished slavery, improved factory conditions, and, most momentous, was in the last stages of the struggle for Reform when Charles began to work there. The struggle succeeded in its immediate objectives, in that the middle-class won a victory over the aristocracy. The plight of the mass of working people was still attended by misery, starvation, unemployment and cholera. There were rick-burnings, riots, and in the North Country the smell of armed rebellion.

Charles, an ardent reformer and alive to the sufferings of poor people, watched this Parliament and was not impressed. The scorn he had quickly conceived for the law applied no less here, with its hot air, obfuscation, bureaucracy and attachment to privilege. What good a few might achieve was apt to be driven out by the mediocre, whom he characterized in *Little Dorrit* as 'tenacious of the utmost deference being shown by everyone, in all things, to Society'.

Night after night, [he wrote in *David Copperfield*] I record predictions that never come to pass, professions that are never fulfilled, explanations that are only meant to mystify. I wallow in words. Britannia, that unfortunate female, is always before me, like a trussed fowl; skewered through and through with office-pens, and bound hand and foot with red tape. I am sufficiently behind the scenes to know the worth of political life. I am quite an Infidel about it, and shall never be converted.

He earned very good money, but worked long hours for it, and took lodgings off the Strand for a while to be near his job. He resigned from the *True Sun*, an ailing paper, after a few months, but on the *Mirror of Parliament* his extraordinary ability soon raised him to a position in which he was trusted to engage other reporters. He had, he said, gone at the job 'with a determination to overcome all the difficulties which fairly lifted me up into that newspaper life, and floated me away over a hundred men's heads'. The memory of the blacking factory was ten years old, though never cancelled. His success at his chosen career was assured. How enviable most young men would have found his life: how little he envied it himself, torn as it was by the caprices of Maria Beadnell, whom he pursued with a romantic intensity that characterized him in every matter.

Chapter Four

Heart of Hearts

MARIA BEADNELL LIVED WITH HER PARENTS AND TWO OLDER sisters in Lombard Street, next to the bank where Mr Beadnell importantly worked. She had dark ringlets, bright eyes, and eyebrows that pouted Charles to distraction. He found her most adorable when, in a particular raspberry-coloured dress with black velvet trimmings at the breast, she was playing the harp. She was still more adroit at plucking the strings of poor Charles's passionate heart. He was seventeen when they met, she a year older, and she charmed him, and laughed and flirted with him and exchanged keepsakes and letters, for four years. More than twenty years later, she declared that she had been in love with him, but by that time he was a famous man and Maria a regretful woman. As a reporter in Doctors' Commons or in Parliament he was not an obviously better match than the other young men who visited the family in Lombard Street, as her parents would have pointed out to her. He was more entertaining perhaps, but with a liveliness, an intensity, a dash, even a suspected radicalism, that unsettled them and endowed him with none of the substance that a banker would wish to find in a young man who pays suit to his daughter.

Charles spent every hour he could in her company, wrote bad poems to her, and envied the dog Daphne whom Maria clasped to her breast. The height of happiness was to be entrusted to match a pair of blue gloves for her; the depth of despair was to be told that her parents were sending her to be 'finished' in Paris for several months. Probably they were encouraged to send her away by the hope that she would forget about him. In romantic novels, such a separation only increases the ardour of expectation. In the case of Maria, it had exactly the effect intended.

At first, when Charles made her acquaintance through his sister Fanny's circle of friends, the Beadnells had seldom taken much notice of so young a man, younger still in appearance. When they did, they were not unkind, but his unimportance was proved by Mrs Beadnell's habit of calling him 'Mr Dickin'. Once, in his frequenting of places where he might chance to meet Maria, he did come across her, enchanting in a green cloak, as she went with her mother and sisters to be fitted for wedding dresses: the eldest sister, Margaret, was to be married to a tea-merchant. (Now there's a young man of substance.) With a high gallant heart, Charles escorted them through the streets until they reached the dressmaker's door. Nervous that he would persist even within the premises, Mrs Beadnell dismissed him, 'And now, Mr Dickin, we'll wish *you* good morning.' But Charles

Opposite: 'The Milkmaid'. Maria Beadnell in rustic dress painted by Henry Austin for Dickens in 1831. Dickens initialled it and gave it to Maria for her album

34

found no fault with the Beadnells, with benign and liberal Mr Beadnell, friendly and caring Mrs Beadnell, sweetly singing Margaret, well-read Anne; and Maria, Maria playing her harp was nothing but an angel.

Gradually the Beadnell parents realized that Charles's attachment to Maria was no passing fancy, and they started to inform themselves about him. His job was not impressive, and the temporary resolve to be an actor must have seemed perfectly bizarre to them. His family had no position, as far as they could discover: and eventually they discovered far enough to learn about John Dickens's spell in the Marshalsea. Still they tolerated his attendance in their home, and sometimes invited him to dinner. For such an occasion, he once composed a long, facetious parody in verse which caricatured, sometimes sharply, those around the dinner-table, to whom he declaimed it after the meal. Polite smiles doubtless greeted it, and puzzled shrugs behind his back; and perhaps embarrassment at the declaration of his love for Maria that he smuggled in, describing himself as

> ... a young Summer Cabbage, without any heart; –
> Not that he's *heartless*, but because, as folks say,
> He lost his a twelve month ago, from last May.

Then, suddenly, this cabbage was 'entirely uprooted' when Maria was sent to Paris. After aching months she came back altered, and gave him no more happiness or hope, only bewilderment, reproaches, cold words and caprices. It was impossible to talk it out with her. Mr Beadnell took care not to leave them alone together. Charles resorted to sending clandestine letters to her, first by means of one of Mr Beadnell's servants, who met him by appointment, then *via* Henry Kolle, a young businessman who was courting Anne Beadnell and was friendly with Charles. But Maria, although she responded to the letters, did so without encouraging Charles's hopes.

A crisis arrived at his twenty-first birthday party. It was held in Bentinck Street, where the Dickens family now resided after a short stay in Fitzroy Street. The lavish provisions and hired waiters must have cheered John Dickens's extravagant heart. 'It was a beautiful party', according to Charles. Late in the evening, after the formal dancing of quadrilles and waltzes, he managed to find a private corner with Maria, and spoke of his feelings for her. She heard him out with 'angelic gentleness' but then, probably using a word borrowed from her parents, she called him a 'boy', and went home. By that 'short and dreadful word' he was pierced as keenly as Coriolanus. He got drunk and woke the next day at noon, now of age, thick-headed and wretched. Whatever Maria's feelings were, we can feel, as Charles must have felt, that she might have temporized on such an occasion.

Still he persisted. He wanted to understand: as though reasons could ease what passes reason. He told her, 'Whatever of fancy, romance, passion, aspiration and determination belong to me I never have separated and never shall separate from

Opposite top: The earliest known portrait of Dickens, painted when he was eighteen by Janet Barrow Opposite bottom: 'Newgate – committed for trial' by Frank Holt Overleaf: 'Covent Garden' by Phoebus Levin, 1864

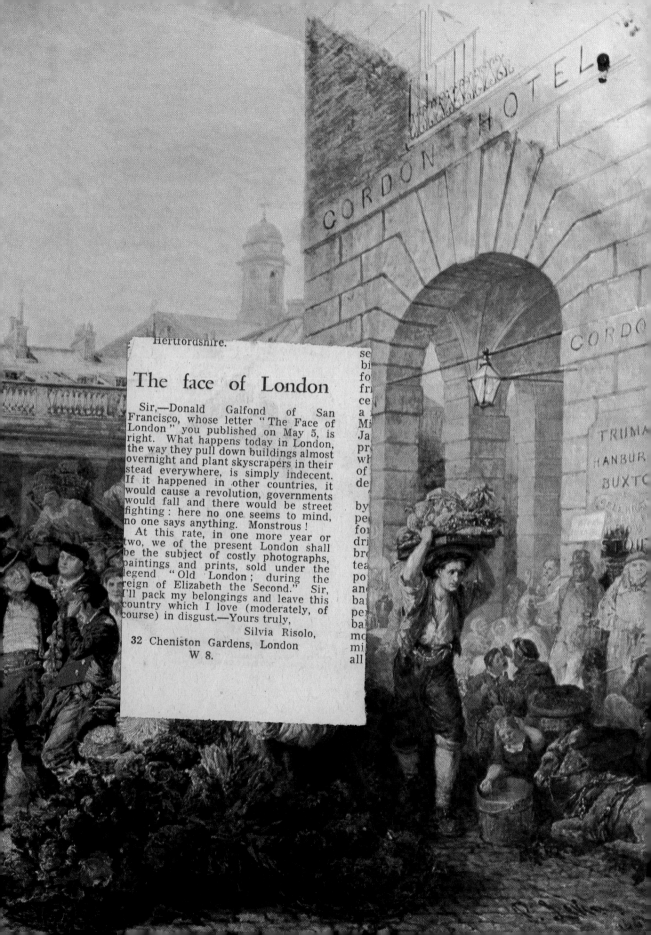

Hertfordshire.

The face of London

Sir,—Donald Galfond of San Francisco, whose letter "The Face of London" you published on May 5, is right. What happens today in London, the way they pull down buildings almost overnight and plant skyscrapers in their stead everywhere, is simply indecent. If it happened in other countries, it would cause a revolution, governments would fall and there would be street fighting: here no one seems to mind, no one says anything. Monstrous!

At this rate, in one more year or two, we of the present London shall be the subject of costly photographs, paintings and prints, sold under the legend "Old London; during the reign of Elizabeth the Second." Sir, I'll pack my belongings and leave this country which I love (moderately, of course) in disgust.—Yours truly,

Silvia Risolo,

32 Cheniston Gardens, London
W 8.

that hard-hearted little woman – you.' Getting no explanation from Maria, he presumed to ask her sister Anne, but she replied, 'I really cannot understand Maria, or venture to take the responsibility of saying what the state of her affections is.' His misery was perplexed by the wiles of Marianne Leigh, Maria's close friend, a mischievous, teasing scandalmonger. She had always sought confidences from him, which he denied her; now she revealed herself as familiar with secrets he had thought he shared only with his beloved, but, having thus proved her intimacy with Maria, went on to tell the abject young man such cruel details of what Maria really thought of him that he could not decide whether she wickedly made them up or was in collusion with Maria to deter him for good.

In the end, a month after the spoiled party, he tied up all Maria's letters in a ribbon coloured the blue of the blue gloves he had matched for her, and sent them back to her with keepsakes she had given him and a letter of his own:

Our meetings of late have been little more than so many displays of heartless indifference on the one hand; while on the other they have never failed to prove a fertile source of wretchedness and misery. . . . Thank God I can claim for myself and *feel* that I deserve the merit of having ever throughout our intercourse acted fairly, intelligently and honourably, under kindness and encouragement one day and a cold change of conduct the next. I have ever been the same. I have ever acted without reserve. Believe me that nothing will ever afford me more real delight than to hear that you, the object of my first and my last love, are happy.

In returning the keepsakes and letters he said, 'I can only wish that I could as easily forget that I ever received them.'

The effort to preserve his dignity would be 'rather touching', as Angus Wilson finds it, if the letter were what it purports to be, a renunciation. In fact it is merely a desperate gambit. He was appealing to a woman's sense of fair play! She kept the game going, having returned the letter to him, by writing to him with just enough hint of regret to sustain his hopes. He was encouraged to persevere, writing back that his love for her had not altered. She returned that letter, too. Undeterred, he invited the Beadnell family to Bentinck Street, where they would witness an evening of amateur theatricals presented by the Dickens family and friends. Charles was to be producer, director, stage-manager, set-designer, effects-man, accordionist, author of the prologue, and leading man in four parts. Often walking past the house in Lombard Street in the small hours, miles out of his way home from Westminster, he would look up at her bedroom window and silently dedicate the whole evening's performance to her – she who would be dazzled by the versatile accomplishments of the man who adored her.

After the show, she said nothing of admiration to him, and little of anything else. Instead he was besieged by Marianne Leigh. A fortnight later, Maria reproached him for having told Marianne intimate details of the years of their romance. The irony was bitter, but Charles could not savour it in his despair: and in his fury,

Opposite: Georgina Hogarth by Daniel Maclise

41

Right: The playbill for the Dickens family's amateur theatricals

Private Theatricals.

STAGE MANAGER, MR. CHARLES DICKENS.

ON SATURDAY EVENING, APRIL 27, 1833,

At Seven o'clock precisely. The performances will commence with

AN INTRODUCTORY PROLOGUE;

THE PRINCIPAL CHARACTERS BY

MR. EDWARD BARROW; MR. MILTON; MR. CHARLES DICKENS; MISS AUSTIN;
AND MISS DICKENS.

IMMEDIATELY AFTER WHICH WILL BE PRESENTED THE OPERA OF

CLARI.

The Duke Vivaldi	MR. BRAMWELL,
Rolamo, a Farmer, (Father to Clari)	MR. C. DICKENS,
Jocoso, (Valet to the Duke)	MR. H. AUSTIN,
Nicolo	MR. MILTON,
Geronio	MR. E. BARROW,
Nimpedo	MR. R. AUSTIN,
Pages to the Duke	MASTERS F. DICKENS & A. DICKENS.
Clari	MISS DICKENS,
Fidalma (her Mother)	MISS L. DICKENS,
Vespina	MISS AUSTIN,
Ninette	MISS OPPENHEIM.

CHARACTERS IN THE EPISODE.

The Nobleman	MR. HENRY KOLLE,
Pelgrino, a Farmer	MR. JOHN DICKENS,
Wife of Pelgrino	MISS URQUHART,
Leoda	MISS OPPENHEIM.

AFTER WHICH THE FAVOURITE INTERLUDE OF

The Married Bachelor.

Sir Charles Courtall	MR. C. DICKENS,
Sharp	MR. JOHN URQUHART,
Lady Courtall	MISS L. DICKENS,
Grace	MISS DICKENS.

TO CONCLUDE WITH THE FARCE OF

Amateurs & Actors.

David Dulcet, Esq. (a Musical Dramatic Amateur, who employs Mr. O. P. Bustle, and attached to Theatricals and Miss Mary Hardacre)	MR. H. AUSTIN,
Mr. O. P. Bustle, (a Provincial Manager, but engaged to superintend some Private Theatricals)	MR. BRAMWELL,
Wing, (a poor Country Actor)	MR. C. DICKENS,
Berry, (an Actor for the heavy Business)	MR. BOSTON,
Elderberry, (a retired Manufacturer, simple in wit and manners, and utterly unacquainted with Theatricals)	MR. J. DICKENS,
Timkins, (Elderberry's Factotum)	MR. R. AUSTIN,
Geoffry Muffincap, (an elderly Charity Boy, let out as a Servant at Bustle's Lodging)	MR. E. BARROW,
Miss Mary Hardacre, (a fugitive Ward of Elderberry's)	MISS DICKENS,
Mrs. Mary Goneril, (a Strolling Tragedy Actress, and a serious evil to her Husband)	MISS OPPENHEIM

The Scenery by Messrs. H. Austin, Milton, H. Kolle, and Assistants.———The Band which will be numerous and
complete, under the direction of Mr. E. Barrow.

J & G. Nichols, Printers, Earl's Court, Cranbourn Street, Soho.

when, having vehemently denied the charge, he returned home and learned from Fanny that she, too, had understood Marianne to be in Charles's confidence. He wrote indignantly to Maria that he would on no account forgive his sister for not having told him before what Marianne was claiming. He was, by now, haplessly struggling in the web which Marianne had perhaps, spiderlike, deliberately woven: Fanny '*knew* what Marianne Leigh had said of *you*; she heard from you what she had said of *me*!' How could Maria have believed Marianne, rather than himself, once so close to her? Was it not Marianne, with her 'duplicity and disgusting falsehood', who had driven the two of them far apart? He would write to Marianne, if Maria had no objections. For himself, 'I have been so long used to inward wretchedness and real, real misery that it matters little, very little to me what others may think or of what becomes of me.'

Below: Maria was the inspiration for Dora Spenlow in Dickens's semi-autobiographical novel David Copperfield, *but unlike David and Dora, Charles and Maria never married*

Maria had no objections, she answered, but might she see the letter before it was sent? She added that he could hardly dislike Marianne as much as he said, since he had, after all, been often noticed in deep conversation with her. Charles was provoked to answer, 'I have borne more from you than I do believe any living creature breathing ever bore from a woman before.' Even her own friends agreed with him about that, he said. The letter was sent to Marianne Leigh, complaining of her 'mischief', and that evening Charles glumly attended a farewell bachelor dinner for Henry Kolle, at whose wedding to Anne Beadnell he was soon to be the best man. Again, he got drunk.

And, yet again, he sought a reconciliation with Maria, offering to forget the bygones. 'I have never loved and I can never love any human creature breathing but yourself.' Maria's reply was written from a small, cold mind, and at last Charles knew that the four years were closed.

To them, later in his life, he attributed 'a habit of suppression which now belongs to me, which I know is no part of my original nature, but which makes me chary of showing my affections, even to my children, except when they are very young'. Instead of the happiness of Chatham, he had been plunged into the rank weeds of Camden Town. Instead of an advancing education, he had been humiliated in the blacking factory. Instead of the substantial background that might well have recommended him to the Beadnells, he had the backcloth of the Marshalsea. Instead of Maria Beadnell, he had a bitter impression on his 'original nature'. All these sorrows inflicted upon him formed a character that, to defend itself in future, would assert its will intimidatingly. He would be nobody's plaything again. In exchange for a lost innocence, he would have his own way. What was necessary, then, was the independence and esteem of success.

Chapter Five

My Eyes So Dimmed

LATE ONE NOVEMBER EVENING IN 1833, DICKENS APPROACHED 'a dark letter-box in a dark office up a dark court in Fleet Street', and into it posted 'with fear and trembling' a long envelope. A few weeks later he entered a bookshop in the Strand and paid half-a-crown for a new issue of the *Monthly Magazine*. A rapid glance through the pages confirmed his trembling hope: there it was in print, 'A Dinner at Poplar Walk', the semi-fictional sketch of London life that he had dropped into the editorial letter-box. He had received no acknowledgement, there was no credit for the author, nor would there be any payment. That did not matter. His own words were in print. For half an hour he walked up and down the empty floor at Westminster Hall, 'my eyes so dimmed with pride and joy that they could not bear the street, and were not fit to be seen.'

More encouraging yet, the magazine wrote to him asking for further contributions. Dickens boasted a little to Henry Kolle and Anne – who might pass the news on to Maria – of the forthcoming 'series' from his pen. 'I am so dreadfully nervous that my hand shakes to such an extent as to prevent my writing a word legibly.' More of his sketches were published in the following months, and soon they were signed with the pseudonym Boz, derived from Moses, the family nickname for his little brother Augustus, which the child mispronounced.

The name of Boz first appeared in August 1834. In that same month Dickens fulfilled another ambition. He was engaged as a parliamentary reporter on a daily newspaper, the *Morning Chronicle*, which in its campaigning liberalism was in rivalry with *The Times*. The pay was less than he had got from *The Mirror of Parliament*, but he would be continuously employed, not only during parliamentary sessions. Indeed, shortly after joining the paper, he was sent to Edinburgh to cover the ceremony in which Earl Grey was given the freedom of the city. No respecter of politicians or pomp, Dickens filed a report from that dignified occasion which described how guests at the ceremonial banquet could not contain their appetites until the great man arrived and started to lay about the tempting food, shouting 'Shame!', with their mouths full, when they saw others doing likewise. It was, Dickens observed, 'one of the few instances on record of a dinner having been virtually concluded before it began'.

The high spirits in such a report reflected Dickens's mood now. So did his manner in London, where he flowered into a dandy, in a blue cloak with velvet facings, and a dashing hat. His energy, long corked up by the melancholy affair with Maria, poured out in good humour and industry. As well as the regular sketches for the *Monthly Magazine*, he started to contribute Street Sketches to the *Morning Chronicle*, where his identity as Boz was now known. People were taking notice of this new writer. The sincerest form of flattery was paid to him in the popular theatres: on one occasion Dickens was sent to review a new farce at the Adelphi, and found himself listening to a rehash of his own work. He was respectfully befriended by a glitteringly successful writer of the time, William Harrison Ainsworth, who introduced his protégé to his own publisher, John Macrone, a silky Manxman.

Left: Dickens posting his first literary contribution in the editor's box

What Dickens called 'the damnable shadow' on his life, his father's improvidence, fell on him again now. John Dickens, once more enmeshed in debts and borrowings, was arrested by one of the dozens of tradesmen to whom he owed overdue bills. Dickens took charge of the situation, paid off the immediate embarrassments, arranged securities for the rest, moved his family into cheaper lodgings, rented rooms for himself and his brother Frederick at Furnival's Inn, Holborn,

Right: Furnival's Inn, Holborn, where Dickens rented rooms for himself and his brother Frederick

and swiftly had the whole family finances straightened out. His efficiency in the matter must have greatly comforted and impressed his parents, for they soon learned to count on it.

It had left him with no money, for the time being, to furnish the rooms at Furnival's Inn, and when the publisher Macrone visited him without appointment, the place was 'uncarpeted and bleak-looking, with a deal table, two or three chairs and a few books, a small boy and Mr Dickens for the contents'.

In October, Dickens shared the popular satisfaction at the sight of the Houses of Parliament burning down. The business of government went on, and after Christmas the *Morning Chronicle* sent him out to cover elections from Ipswich to Exeter. It was pouring with rain in Devon, and Dickens could note down Lord John Russell's speech only by courtesy of a handkerchief that two colleagues held over his notebook, 'after the manner of a state canopy in an ecclesiastical procession'. Then there was the question, in those pre-telephone days, of getting the copy back to London, and back sooner than the rival papers – in particular

The Times, which was boasting that it was always first with the news. It turned into a horse race, literally, over a two-hundred-mile mud-track. Dickens 'bribed the post-boys tremendously' and won the race at a rheumatic cost to himself. He was complimented on the accuracy as well as the priority of his report; though not, of course, by *The Times*, which instead described its rival organ as 'that squirt of filthy water'. The *Chronicle* complacently answered, 'The poor old *Times*, in its imbecilic ravings, resembles those unfortunate wretches whose degraded prostitution is fast approaching neglect and disgust.' No nonsense about 'dog don't eat dog' in those days. Dog gobbled down every canine morsel it could snatch.

The *Morning Chronicle* had inaugurated a sister paper, the *Evening Chronicle*, and at once Dickens was set to writing more Street Sketches for it. He felt entitled to ask for an increase in his salary. When it was granted he informed his first publisher, the *Monthly Magazine*, that he could not continue to write for it unpaid, and that series was concluded. After twenty sketches for the *Evening Chronicle* Dickens went on, without pausing, to write twelve more for *Bell's Life in London*. All the while he continued his regular work as a reporter for the *Morning Chronicle*.

By now Dickens was a visitor to William Harrison Ainsworth's dinner parties in Willesden, where he met the celebrated artist George Cruikshank and the younger Daniel Maclise, the politicians Benjamin Disraeli and Edward Bulwer-Lytton, and other literary lights. One evening he walked home to Holborn with the publisher Macrone, who made the suggestion that Dickens's 'capital' sketches

Below left: William Harrison Ainsworth Below right: A self-portrait of George Cruikshank

49

*Opposite: The young
Charles Dickens by George
Cruikshank*

should be collected as a book, to be illustrated by Cruikshank. He would need to write some additional sketches to fill the two volumes that Macrone projected. Dickens, elated, knew he would have no trouble in doing that. His brain was teeming with ideas.

His heart, too, was busy. The editor of the *Evening Chronicle*, George Hogarth, a Scotsman who had been a friend of Sir Walter Scott, took a personal interest in Dickens, inviting him home to Chelsea. There he had formed an attachment with Hogarth's eldest daughter, Catherine, who was nineteen, and it was understood that they would marry when he had paid off the debts that his father's recent foibles had entailed upon him.

Eighteen months after his final break with Maria and his trembling visit to Fleet Street to post that first sketch in the dark letter-box, he was betrothed, established at the top of his first profession, and on the verge of a literary career. It was a heady rise, and his prodigious energy was in full spate.

He was off to Bristol, reporting a political meeting for the *Morning Chronicle*, and scooped *The Times* again by hiring a post-chaise and four as far as Marlborough, in which he wrote up his shorthand notes 'on the palm of my hand, by the light of a dark lantern . . . galloping through a wild country', then handing the report to a rider on horseback. In London he visited Newgate prison to gather copy for an additional sketch in the book – after his early experience of the Marshalsea, all his life he wanted to see inside the prison of anywhere he visited, in Europe and America. Then he was in Kettering, where he was shocked by the violence of the hustings, where horsemen slashed their way through a crowd, pistols were waved around, claques were rigged, and drunken brawls were a normal feature of the electoral scene. And back to London, where he won the esteem of his journalistic colleagues by successfully leading a strike of the *Morning Chronicle* reporters against a new management policy. At the same time he was supervising the publication of his first book with a self-assurance which was astonishing in a fledgling author. Impatient to see Cruikshank's engravings, he told Macrone that that celebrated illustrator 'requires the spur'. He also took on yet another commission, the libretto for an operetta by John Hullah, a composer friend of Fanny's, but informed Hullah that he was going to write something quite different from what the composer had in mind. It was the self-assurance of a man who had promised himself fame and success, and now found the promise coming true with intoxicating speed.

Sketches by Boz was published on Dickens's twenty-fourth birthday and was reprinted a few months later. The reviews were warm with approval, praising, as George Hogarth did, a 'close observer of character and manners, with a strong sense of the ridiculous'. But there was a power of indignation in the book, too, at 'the vices and wretchedness which abound in this vast city . . . producing tears as well as laughter'.

50

Charles Dickens —

G. Cruikshank

London, Published June 2nd 1879, by Frank Kerslake, 22 Coventry Street, W.

Better than any review was an invitation from the publishers Chapman and Hall to write a comic book in twenty serial instalments. It would add twelve thousand words a month to his formidable workload, but £14 a month to his income, enabling him and Catherine to marry. It was too tempting to resist.

William Hall called on him to arrange the terms, and with joy Dickens recognized the man who, a bookseller two years earlier, had sold Dickens the copy of the *Monthly Magazine* in which his first sketch had appeared. What Chapman and Hall proposed was that Dickens should write a series of comic sporting stories to accompany illustrations by the popular artist Robert Seymour. What Dickens answered was that he would write a series of comic episodes'set in any scenes that he himself chose, and Seymour was to illustrate these. Whatever Chapman and Hall, and Seymour, thought of that proposition, Dickens added, he was afraid that he would certainly find himself doing what *he* wanted. The publishers were won by Dickens's cool assurance, and Seymour, a splenetic soul, had to put up with it. Within the week of Hall's visit, Dickens was writing to him, 'Pickwick is begun in all his might and glory.'

Chapter Six

Dearest Mouse

DICKENS'S SELF-ASSURANCE AND DETERMINATION TO HAVE HIS own way extended to his view of marriage. Having danced attendance on Maria Beadnell and suffered a painful rejection for it, he would not dance for anyone again.

Catherine Hogarth, a languorous, plump woman, had none of the skittish spirits of Maria. But there was in her a tendency to moods of depression, and at such times the demands her petulance made upon Dickens were reminiscent of Maria's caprices. He handled them in a very different manner. Soon after their engagement, he had occasion to write her a letter of reprimand:

My Dear Catherine,

It is with the greatest pain that I sit down before I go to bed tonight, to say one word which can bear the appearance of unkindness or reproach; But I owe a duty to myself as well as to you, and as I am wild enough to think that an engagement of even three weeks might pass without any such display as you have favoured me with thrice already, I am the more strongly induced to discharge it.

The sudden and uncalled for coldness with which you treated me before I left last night surprised and deeply hurt me – surprised because I could not have believed that such sullen and inflexible obstinacy could exist in the breast of any girl in whose heart love had found a place; and hurt me because I feel for you far more than I have ever professed, and feel a slight from you more than I can tell....

If a *hasty* temper produces this strange behaviour, acknowledge it when I give you the opportunity – not once or twice, but again and again. If a feeling of you know not what – a capricious restlessness of you can't tell what, and a desire to teaze, you don't know why, give rise to it – overcome it; it will never make you more amiable, I more fond, or either of us more happy.

Catherine's note in reply confessed to all her fiancé's reproaches, and begged for pardon and his renewed love. Dickens magnanimously granted it, but felt obliged to draw a lesson for her from the 'amiable and excellent feeling' in her letter:

If you would only determine to *shew* the same affection and kindness to me, when you feel disposed to be ill-tempered, I declare unaffectedly I should have no one solitary fault to find with you. Your asking me to love you 'once more' is quite unnecessary – *I have NEVER* ceased to love you for one moment since I knew you; nor *shall I.*

The incident was over (though it recurred), and the die was cast: gentle, firm mastery would be Dickens's tone to Catherine, and she would respect it and do her best to rein in her sulks.

54

There were light-hearted pleasures in the engagement, too. On one celebrated occasion, the Hogarth family were sitting quietly at home when, as Dickens related it to his daughter Mary, 'a young man dressed as a sailor jumped in at the window, danced a hornpipe, whistling the tune, jumped out again, and a few minutes later Charles Dickens walked gravely in at the door, as if nothing had happened, shook hands all round, and then, at the sight of their puzzled faces, burst into a roar of laughter.' His letters to Catherine contained many endearments; she was his 'dearest Kate', 'dearest mouse', 'darling Tatie', 'dearest darling Pig'. He would complain that he had not seen her 'since seven o'clock yesterday evening'. Sometimes she would call at his room to have breakfast with him, accompanied by her sister Mary, who was five years younger and doted upon her admired brother-in-law-to-be. He took them and sometimes others of the Hogarth family on visits to the theatre, where he was making a name not only as a critic but also as the author of the forthcoming libretto, and of a one-act farce he had undertaken to adapt from one of his sketches.

With all the work he had taken on, however, which often found him still wearily under his lamp an hour or two past midnight, he was obliged to spend less of his time with Catherine than she would have liked; a prolonged cold and a recurrence of his kidney spasm were symptoms of his exhaustion, and also kept him from her side. She complained, saying that his devotion to work made her 'coss'. Dickens replied:

Left: Mrs Charles Dickens (Kate) in 1842

You may be disappointed:—I would rather you would—at not seeing me; but you cannot feel vexed at my doing my best with the stake I have to play for—you and a home for both of us. . . . I perceive you have not yet subdued one part of your disposition—your distrustful feelings and want of confidence . . . I love you far too well to feel hurt by what in any one else would have annoyed me greatly.

and in another letter answering the same complaint:

If the representations I have so often made to you, about my working as a duty, and not as a pleasure, be not sufficient to keep you in the good humour, which you, of all people in the world should preserve—why then my dear, you must be out of temper, and there is no help for it.

Dickens was proud to be able to describe his future wife as 'the daughter of a gentleman who had recently distinguished himself by a celebrated work on music, who was the most intimate friend and companion of Sir Walter Scott, and one of the most eminent of the literati of Edinburgh'. That pride was expressed in a letter to his uncle, Thomas Culliford Barrow; Dickens regretted that he would be unable to introduce Catherine to him, for his uncle refused to meet John Dickens, and Charles, though protesting that his uncle had misjudged his father, was not willing to compromise his filial loyalty.

The wedding took place at St Luke's Church, Chelsea, on 2 April 1836, two days after the publication of the first instalment of *Pickwick Papers*. Apart from the best man—Thomas Beard, a colleague of Dickens's—and the publisher Macrone, only the Hogarth and Dickens families attended the ceremony and the wedding breakfast at the Hogarths' home. Harry Burnett, who was engaged to Fanny, remembered that 'A few common, pleasant things were said, healths were drunk with a very few words', and everyone seemed happy, 'not the least so Dickens and his young girlish wife'. There was time for only a one-week honeymoon, which they spent in a cottage in the countryside of Dickens's childhood, near Chatham. Then they moved back to Furnival's Inn, where, assisted by the women of the Hogarth family, Dickens had furnished his three bachelor rooms in a style befitting a married couple.

With them would live Mary Hogarth, a merry, sweet and beautiful girl of sixteen, to whom both were devoted. It was, perhaps, an odd decision to make, to start married life with an adolescent companion. But as far as Dickens was concerned, marriage would be a sensible, domestic arrangement. After a day's work, dedicated to the 'advancement and happiness' of his wife, he would relax by the fireside and explain 'rationally what I have been doing'. Never by that fireside would he breathe a word of what was deepest in him, beyond reason; no mention to Catherine of the blacking factory, nor of Maria Beadnell. That 'habit of suppression' that he attributed to his suffering years with Maria would prevent his marriage from exceeding a friendly companionship in which he was to be the master.

Chapter Seven

Pickwick Triumphant

IN CONTRAST TO *Sketches by Boz*, THE FIRST INSTALMENT OF *Pickwick* was disappointingly received in spite of energetic publicizing by Chapman and Hall. Reviewers were cool about an 'exhausted comicality' in the satire and sales were thin.

Dickens gave no sign of being daunted. He busied himself with getting the illustrations for the second instalment just as he wanted them. The artist, Robert Seymour, had had trouble in the first instalment, when he produced a sketch of Pickwick as a tall, thin man and the publishers had said no, no, Pickwick must be fat, 'good humour and flesh had always gone together since the days of Falstaff'. Seymour, thoroughly cross to be dictated to about what had initially been his own project, was now told that his work for the second instalment would have to be done again. He agreed to meet Dickens, for the first time, to talk it all over. The meeting at Furnival's Inn was short. Seymour, politely told by the young author that he must do as he was asked, offered no constructive suggestions. He went away to re-engrave the plates, and spoiled one of them. He engraved it again, successfully, then picked up a shotgun and blew his brains out.

Chapman and Hall agreed to continue publication with a new illustrator to be chosen by Dickens. Cruikshank was too busy with other work. Among the applicants whom Dickens interviewed was a very tall young artist called William Makepeace Thackeray (he would later illustrate his own book, *Vanity Fair*), who

Right: An anonymous engraving of Hablôt Knight Browne, the illustrator of many of Dickens's novels under the name 'Phiz'

58

imagined that he had been chosen and celebrated in sausage-and-mash with a shy, young fellow artist, Hablôt Knight Browne. Another was R. W. Buss, a painter who had exhibited at the Royal Academy but who did not know how to etch. He put aside all his work to concentrate on learning the technique, understanding that he was commissioned for *Pickwick*, and was furious when his plates were rejected. By now the choice had been made: Hablôt Knight Browne, later known to the readers of Dickens as 'Phiz'. Whether he bought Thackeray a sausage-and-mash in return is not known.

He had lately worked with Dickens for the first time, illustrating a political pamphlet, *Sunday Under Three Heads*. Dickens had dashed it off as an enraged reply to a Sabbatarian Bill in Parliament that would have prohibited all public recreation on Sundays, and the sale of food – principally aiming at the excursions that working people took after six days of labour. The sponsor of the Bill was Sir Andrew Agnew

Baronets [Dickens wrote] eat pretty comfortable dinners all the week through, and cannot be expected to understand what people feel, who only have a meat dinner on one day out of every seven ... it is customary to affect a deference for the motives of those who advocate these measures, and a respect for the feelings by which they are actuated. They do not deserve it. If they legislate in ignorance, they are criminal and dishonest; if they do so with their eyes open, they commit wilful injustice; in either case, they bring religion into contempt.

Instead, Dickens urged, let ordinary people enjoy themselves on Sundays, with family outings on the river, walks, cricket matches, and let the museums and galleries be opened for them on the one day they could visit them. Envious Sabbatarian bigotry could only drive such people into the condition of those wretches who filled the gin-palaces in Seven Dials.

As well as that pamphlet, Dickens was concurrently at work on the libretto, the farce, his roving reports for the *Morning Chronicle* (including the trial in which the Prime Minister, Lord Melbourne, was alleged to have had scandalous relations with the Hon. Mrs Caroline Norton), a new series of sketches for Macrone, and, before all, the monthly instalments of *Pickwick*. He was in fact writing eight pages more for each instalment now, the number of illustrations having been reduced during the search for an artist to replace Seymour: Dickens had, characteristically, obtained an increased fee from Chapman and Hall in return. An understanding they had, however, that his fee would be further increased after four or five instalments had established *Pickwick*'s popularity, was now looking poorly. With a few exceptions, the reviewers were still not impressed and sales were meagre. Dickens gladly took on yet more work when Macrone offered him £200 (with more to come if there was a second edition) for a novel provisionally entitled *Gabriel Vardon, the Locksmith of London*, and to be written in the space of a few months.

Macrone, by now a family friend, made another interesting offer: to give Dickens's fifteen-year-old brother Frederick an accounts job in his publishing house. Mindful of his own interrupted education, Dickens hesitated, but decided that further schooling for Fred now would be 'only so much waste time'. He made it a condition, however, that he would see Fred every tea-time to assure himself that his brother continued to study. Whether John Dickens was consulted is doubtful. The incident was another example of Charles's acceptance that he would be responsible for the whole family's welfare.

It was when Mr Pickwick met Sam Weller, cleaning shoes in a yard not far from the Marshalsea, that the fortunes of the book turned, and with them Dickens's own fortune. That fourth instalment captivated the market. Monthly sales rose from four hundred to forty thousand. It was read upstairs and downstairs, by judges on the bench and the cleaners after them. 'All the boys and girls talk his fun – the boys in the streets', wrote Mary Russell Mitford, 'and yet they who are of the highest taste like it most.' Critics spoke of Dickens as another Cervantes, poor people shared a shilling copy and read it aloud in groups. A clergyman, having consoled a sick man, heard him mutter behind his back, 'Well, thank God, Pickwick will be out in ten days anyway!' No hat or coat, cigar or cane, plagiaristic paper or play, could be sold but with a Pickwick tag. It was 'Pickwick Triumphant', as Dickens announced. Chapman and Hall were selling the back numbers in thousands, and more than doubled their fee to Dickens.

He was the sudden lion of the town. Offers poured in. Dickens undertook to write yet more sketches. Then he agreed on a children's book, but cancelled it when the publisher Richard Bentley offered him £400 each for two new novels. Dickens successfully stuck out for £500 each, on the grounds of 'the rapid sale of *everything* I have yet touched' and 'the anxiety I should feel to make it a work on which I might build my fame'. From a summer holiday in Petersham he was constantly dashing back to London to assist at rehearsals and see how his publishing affairs were going. The one-act farce, entitled *The Strange Gentleman*, scored a success when it opened in September 1836, though its conventional business must have disappointed *Pickwick* readers. The new collections of *Sketches* was going to press: Cruikshank, working on the illustrations, declared that he also wished to improve the text, here and there. 'I have long believed Cruikshank to be mad', Dickens told Macrone, and suggested that the 'improvements' be preserved as 'curiosities of literature'. Or perhaps Cruikshank should be altogether dropped in favour of Phiz. Cruikshank it was, however, who illustrated the first volume of the new *Sketches*: the projected second volume Dickens had no time to prepare, owing to pressure of work and a fortnight ill in bed.

No young lion escapes jealous darts, and Dickens ran into a hail of them when the operetta, *The Village Coquettes*, opened in December. The writer George Augustus Sala, then ten years old, was backstage while his mother played the

lead, and later he described how Dickens looked to him: 'a very young gentleman with long brown hair falling in silky masses over his temples ... dressed up to the very height of the existing fashion', the eyes 'full of power and strong will, and with a touching expression of sweetness and kindliness on his lips'. Dickens was unconventional enough to respond to the cries of 'Boz!' by actually appearing on the stage and taking a bow. The reviewers were 'utterly amazed' at so 'extremely ill-advised' a gesture. 'When will this ridiculous nonsense end?' they asked. There was a general feeling that the operetta – not a distinguished work, in spite of the overweening praise of those who produced it – was cashing in on the fame of the author of *Pickwick*. 'Some critics in the gallery were said to have expected Sam Weller', one paper wrote. There were suspicions that a claque had been arranged.

It has been argued that Dickens, always an alert publicist, was simply attempting to promote the production and his own reputation. He cared nothing for those who thought his appearance on stage undignified; just as he scorned those who criticized him for permitting his work to be serialized, 'a low, cheap form of publication', instead of issuing it in sober, calf covers. He did not want an audience limited to those who could afford a guinea and a half. He wanted everyone to share his work: and besides, it made business sense. However, business sense was, surely, not what sent him on to the stage of the St James's Theatre, but his adoration of being at the centre of the theatrical tumult, a lifelong love. 'It might not be in the best of taste to behave in this way,' Christopher Hibbert remarks in his biography, 'but then, as George Santayana has said, Dickens had more genius than taste.'

The limelight never left him. The Pickwick mania was unparalleled. 'If I were to live a hundred years', Dickens wrote to Chapman and Hall, 'and write three works in each, I should never be so proud of any of them as I am of Pickwick, feeling as I do, that it has made its own way, and hoping, as I must own I do hope, that long after my hand is withered as the pens it held, Pickwick will be found on many a dusty shelf with many a better work.' His satisfaction went deeper than that of a young man who has scored a sensational success. The form of that success, a 'realist fairy tale' as the book has been called, answered to what was deepest in Dickens. Starting from the loved books of his childhood – 'I have sustained my own idea of Roderick Random for a month at a stretch' – with the idea of a picaresque series of adventures, and using the experiences that he had suffered as a boy, then seen as a reporter, his satire transcends his personal experience, copes with all that the world can do to a man, by laughing at it.

Chapter Eight

Their Secret Places

RICHARD BENTLEY, A SHORT, FLORID MAN AND A DARING publisher, wanted to launch a new monthly magazine, *Bentley's Miscellany*. He offered Dickens over £40 a month to edit it and contribute sixteen pages of his own work.

Elated with his powers, Dickens had been finding it hard to refuse any offer. Accepting this one from Bentley – for whom he had also contracted to write two novels – he was in a position to trim his less attractive commitments: chiefly, the tiring and time-consuming job with the *Morning Chronicle*. How glad he would be never to sit through another tedious debate in the Commons.

The newspaper, naturally sorry to lose its star reporter, replied ungraciously to Dickens's letter of resignation. Stung by their ingratitude for all his unstinting efforts – 'I have been, in my time, belated on miry by-roads, towards the small hours, in a wheelless carriage, with exhausted horses and drunken postboys, and have got back in time for publication' – Dickens wrote back an acid note: and it was typical that, when the paper reasonably pointed out that Dickens owed them some gratitude, too, and tried to make amends with a favourable notice of the first issue of the *Miscellany*, Dickens answered, 'I cannot retract one syllable.' Years later, he could look back nostalgically at his reporting days and praise the *Chronicle*'s generosity to him; but his temper, now, was always as fast up and unremitting as Coriolanus's.

It flared up again, soon afterwards, against Macrone, his first publisher and hitherto a close friend. Dickens thought he had reason to assume that his signed agreement to write *Gabriel Vardon* for Macrone had been set aside, but Macrone, probably envious of Bentley, now accused Dickens of breaking his contract, and dragged their joint friend Ainsworth into the argument. Meanwhile, he stoked up his case by advertising the forthcoming appearance of the novel, which Dickens had no intention of writing, nor the time. An advertisement was even sent to Chapman and Hall for inclusion in *Pickwick*, though at Dickens's request it was not printed. Eventually an agreement was reached: Macrone would relinquish his claim on *Gabriel Vardon* in return for being allowed to buy the copyright of all the *Sketches by Boz* he had published, at an outright price of £100. Dickens was bitter when he reflected that he had made, in all, some £400 from the books, and Macrone ten times as much.

But everything else was going splendidly as 1836, a marvellous year in Dickens's life, huddled down for Christmas. *Pickwick* continued to be a monthly triumph.

Extraordinary Gazette.

SPEECH OF HIS MIGHTINESS

ON OPENING THE SECOND NUMBER

OF

BENTLEY'S MISCELLANY,

EDITED BY "BOZ."

On Wednesday, the first of February, "the House"
(of Bentley) met for the despatch of business, in pur-
suance of the Proclamation inserted by authority in
all the Morning, Evening, and Weekly Papers, ap-
pointing that day for the publication of the Second
Number of the Miscellany, edited by "Boz."

*Left: An advertising
circular composed by
Dickens for* Bentley's
Miscellany *in February
1837. The design by Phiz
shows Dickens, the editor,
leading a stout porter who
carries a huge quantity of
the magazines*

Dickens energetically attended to all his duties on the *Miscellany*, stamping his character upon it and proudly commissioning contributions from leading writers of the day, whom he met at a series of literary dinners at Bentley's office in New Burlington Street. On such occasions Dickens 'kept very quiet, purposely. Since I have been a successful author, I have seen how much ill-will and jealousy there is afloat, and have acquired an excellent character as a quiet, modest fellow. I like to assume a virtue, though I have it not.' There was a series of parties, at which he sometimes drank too much. Often he was accompanied by Mary Hogarth, for Kate was expecting their first child, and, unlike Dickens's own mother, thought it wise not to go out gravidly dancing. 'Boz seems not to be sleeping', an acquaintance noted. 'His name appears to irradiate three publishers' lists. How does his pretty little sister-in-law get on? She is a sweet interesting creature. I wonder some two-legged monster does not carry her off. It might save many a yonker losing his night's rest.'

On Christmas Day Ainsworth, who had introduced Dickens to his first publisher, Macrone, now performed an even more significant introduction – to John Forster, the critic of the *Examiner*. Forster was slightly younger than Dickens, but did not seem it. His weighty, mandarin presence, with a north-country assertiveness, contrasted with Dickens's youthful eagerness. He became Dickens's closest friend for life, and survived him to write the standard biography. Though a particular friend to Dickens, he was strenuous in helping other writers he approved of, counselling them in the capacity of a good literary agent, before that profession had been invented. 'Whenever anybody is in a scrape we all fly to him for refuge', Thackeray said. 'He is omniscient and works miracles.'

Dickens's first child was born in Furnival's Inn on Twelfth Night, attended by his grandmother. He was named for his father. 'I shall never be so happy again as in those chambers three storeys high – never if I roll in wealth and fame', Dickens wrote, with more prescience than he knew. Kate took some time to recover from the birth, and Dickens himself was plagued by headaches from overwork, so they took a holiday, with the baby and Mary, in the Medway cottage where they had spent their honeymoon. Meanwhile house agents were instructed to find a more suitable family home than the three-room chambers.

A few days before the birth, the first issue of the *Miscellany* had appeared, and soon Bentley was 'inundated with orders'. The second issue, in February, carried the opening instalment of a new novel, *Oliver Twist*, illustrated by Cruikshank.

The vast audience that *Pickwick* was commanding took to the new work, too, but it was certainly a departure from the merry world of Samuel Pickwick and Sam Weller, though not so much from some of the *Sketches*. Only a few traces of the earlier loving, loved satire remain: instead, a savage indignation expresses itself in melodrama, pathos and sarcasm. It was an indignation that had been bred through endless hours in Parliament listening to well-fed men debate the problem

of the poor. 'When poor law reform is being discussed', Sydney Smith once remarked, 'every man rushes to the press with his small morsel of imbecility, and is not easy till he sees his impertinence stitched in blue covers.' But nothing could be more pertinent to the recent new Poor Law than the picture Dickens painted of the workhouses, slums, and thieves' dens that he had seen for himself, including the original of Fagin, in his years of walking the breadth of London, and feared for himself in his time at the blacking factory. The observation, which Dickens carefully justified by checking statistical reports, is the work of a reporter, and it produced the lurid world that epitomizes what we now mean by 'Dickensian'. The spiritual force of the book was an imaginary autobiography.

In Kent, Dickens continued to work as hard as ever on the monthly instalments of *Pickwick* and *Oliver Twist*, on editing the *Miscellany*, and on another one-act farce, which was produced in March 1837, but won small success.

Later that month the family moved into their new house just north of Gray's

Below: Cruikshank's preliminary drawing for Fagin in the condemned cell in Oliver Twist

Inn, in Doughty Street, a private road with a gate at each end locked at night by a liveried porter. There were twelve rooms, enough to allow young Fred to add his high spirits to the household, and to entertain often in the evenings. Henry Burnett, Fanny's husband, has left a description of one evening there:

Mrs Charles Dickens, my wife and myself were sitting round the fire cosily enjoying a chat, when Dickens, for some purpose, came suddenly into the room. 'What, you here!' he exclaimed, 'I'll bring down my work.' It was his monthly portion of 'Oliver Twist' for Bentley's. In a few minutes he returned, manuscript in hand, and while he was pleasantly discoursing he employed himself in carrying to the corner of the room a little table, at which he seated himself and recommenced his writing. We, at his bidding, went on talking our 'little nothings', – he, every now and then (the feather of his pen still moving rapidly from side to side), put in a cheerful interlude. It was interesting to watch, upon the sly, the mind and the muscles working (or, if you please, *playing*) in company, as new thoughts were being dropped upon the paper. And to note the work-

Left: 'The Burglary' in Oliver Twist *by George Cruikshank*

ing brow, the set of mouth, with the tongue tightly pressed against the closed lips, as was his habit.

Pickwick's first birthday was celebrated by Chapman and Hall with a dinner and an *ex gratia* gift of £500, in token of the unlooked-for fortune that the work had brought them all. There were other cheerful dinners, when Dickens sang comic songs and exercised his talent of mimicry. There were walks and horse-rides with Ainsworth. There were unlimited prospects. And so, exactly as in one of his own novels, there was a tragic turn of fate. With 'awful suddenness', Mary Hogarth died at the age of seventeen.

Dickens, Kate and Mary came in from the theatre one evening, and Mary 'went upstairs to bed at about one o'clock in perfect health and her usual delightful spirits'. No sooner had she shut the bedroom door behind her than Dickens heard her give a choking cry. He rushed up, found her gasping, and sent Fred for a doctor. But nothing could be done. The next afternoon

> she sank under the attack and died – died in such a calm and gentle sleep, that although I had held her in my arms for some time before, when she was certainly living (for she swallowed a little brandy from my hand) I continued to support her lifeless form, long after her soul had fled to Heaven.... The very last words she whispered were of me.... They think her heart was diseased.

Below: No. 48 Doughty Street, Mecklenburgh Square – the Dickens's home from 1837–9

Dickens took a ring from her lifeless finger, put it on his own, and it remained there until he died.

Mrs Hogarth fainted at her daughter's death and did not come to for a week. Kate, needing to console her mother as well as herself, found a new strength which Dickens could only admire, but soon afterwards she had a miscarriage.

Remembering Mary's 'sweet face and winning smile, guileless heart and affectionate nature', Dickens declared, in many black-bordered letters, that the misery was inconceivable. She 'had been the grace and life of our home. We might have known that we were too happy together to be long without a change.' 'I have lost the dearest friend I ever had ... the dear girl whom I loved, after my wife, more deeply and fervently than anyone on earth.' 'I could have better spared a much nearer relation or an older friend, for she has been to us what we can never replace.' 'Words cannot describe the pride I felt in her, and the devoted attachment I bore her.' As well as the ring, he kept her clothes, to look upon as they 'moulder away in their secret places'. He wrote an inscription for her tombstone, and hoped to be buried beside her. Looking at a lock of her hair, six months after her death, he wrote,

> I wish you could know how I weary now for the three rooms in Furnival's Inn, and how I miss that pleasant smile and those sweet words which, bestowed upon our evening's work, in our merry banterings round the fire, were more precious to me than the applause of a whole world could be. I can recall everything we said and did in those days.

Some years later, he wrote to Mrs Hogarth,

After she died I dreamed of her every night for many months, sometimes as a spirit, sometimes as a living creature, never with any of the bitterness of my real sorrow, but always with a kind of quiet happiness, which became so pleasant to me that I never lay down at night without a hope of the vision coming back in one shape or other. And so it did. I went down into Yorkshire, and finding it still present to me in a strange scene and a strange bed, I could not help mentioning the circumstances in a note I wrote home to Kate. From that moment I have never dreamed of her once, though she is so much in my thoughts at all times (especially when I am successful and have prospered in anything) that the recollection of her is an essential part of my being, and is as inseparable from my being as the beating of my heart is.

Left: Mary Hogarth in a posthumous portrait by Phiz

The agony that Mary's death caused in Dickens clearly goes deeper than the loss of even the dearest friend, and anyone who wishes to may speculate, as many have, on what his deepest feelings for her were, deeper perhaps than he dared recognize himself. While she lived, he could only repress such feelings. After her death, in idealizing her – 'I solemnly believe that so perfect a creature never breathed' – he was idealizing the feelings she had aroused in him. No sexual union is as lastingly sweet as the one that is only imagined. It remains purified of shame, remorse, or disappointment.

In Dickens, the verifiable effects were of two sorts, in his marriage and his writing. Kate, who had never had a 'cross word or angry look' with her sister, was no match for an idealized Mary, and the unequal comparison contributed to the erosion of their marriage. In his novels, Dickens never fails to sentimentalize the virginal girl. Most notably of all, Little Nell is 'a creature fresh from the hand of God', and Dickens 'trembled' as the need to describe her death approached. 'I am the wretchedest of the wretched', he said. 'It casts the most horrible shadow upon me, and it is as much as I can do to keep moving at all. . . . Dear Mary died yesterday, when I think of this sad story.'

Immediately after the death, Dickens was unable to write a word, save in letters. Both *Pickwick* and *Oliver Twist* were suspended for an instalment, with a brief explanation to the reader. For a fortnight, Dickens and Kate sought rest and quiet at a small, ancient farm in Hampstead, visited only by a few close friends.

He visited her grave but relinquished his hope of joining Mary there, offering the space to the Hogarth family when they suffered a double bereavement some years later. It was a noble gesture and a painful one. 'I cannot bear the thought of being excluded from her dust', he said. 'It seems like losing her a second time.' He consoled himself by going to the cemetery when the grave was re-opened and gazing for the last time at Mary's coffin.

Chapter Nine

A Strong Spice
of the Devil

'THE LABOUR OF BEING IDLE', EVEN BRIEFLY, WAS AN ORDEAL for Dickens, and now that Mary was not there he could not easily relax in Doughty Street. His favourite recreation was to clear his brain by exhausting his body with exercise. He took long, fast walks and vigorous rides on horseback, most often with Forster as companion. After a morning's work, having ordered horses at the door for eleven o'clock, off they would go, through Richmond and Twickenham, out to Windsor, or up to Hampstead Heath, to eat at a 'good 'ous where we can have a red-hot chop for dinner, and a glass of good wine', and gallop back through Barnes, or Acton, or Stanmore.

Above: Two sketches of John Forster by Daniel Maclise

There was a feverishness, too, in his social life. At dinners and suppers, in clubs, literary societies, and at Doughty Street, he frequently met the other leading writers and artists of the time, as well as his older friends. There was the great actor-manager Macready, the whimsical essayist Leigh Hunt, Thackeray, now emerging as a novelist, the luxurious Edward Bulwer-Lytton, and a host of others whose names are now seldom remembered but who made up the tissue of wit, magnanimity and jealousy in London then.

In November 1837 a memorable banquet was given by Chapman and Hall to celebrate the completion of *Pickwick Papers*; before '*the* toast of the evening' the head waiter 'placed a glittering temple of confectionery on the table, beneath the canopy of which stood a little figure of the illustrious Mr Pickwick.' The publishers also gave Dickens another cheque, for £750. In all, he had made at most £3000 from the work (at a time when a middle-class income was between £150 and £400). Chapman and Hall had made five times as much from their speculative investment, but their sensible policy of friendly gifts kept the relationship warm. Under pressure from Forster, they conceded Dickens a one-third share in the copyright and profits of *Pickwick*, effective from five years after publication.

They were also loyal allies to him in the difficulties he had with other publishers. Macrone stirred up the *Sketches by Boz* argument again when he proposed to re-issue the book in monthly instalments wrapped in green covers very like those of *Pickwick*. Having bought the copyright for £100, he had already made thousands from it, and now, in making yet more, threatened the rest of Dickens's continuing work. With advice from Forster, Dickens finally accepted an offer from Chapman and Hall to repurchase the copyright and share the cost and future income with Dickens. Macrone stuck out for £2250, and got it. Dickens's indignation can be imagined: yet a few months later Macrone died suddenly and Dickens was in the forefront of a plan to assist his family with a benefit volume of work donated by writers connected with the publishing house.

Dickens now had the means to enjoy holidays, on the French and Belgian coasts, and in Broadstairs, Brighton, Twickenham. His first trip abroad was full of delightful observations.

A gentleman in a blue surtout and silken berlins accompanied us from the hotel and acted as curator. He even waltzed with a very smart lady (just to shew us, condescendingly, how it ought to be done), and waltzed elegantly too. We rang for slippers after we came back, and it turned out that this gentleman was the Boots. Isn't this French?

'Phiz' accompanied Dickens and Kate on that holiday, and all their hide-aways were visited by a stream of friends coming down for a few days. Dickens encouraged them to visit: when he was not at his writing, the thought of which possessed him throughout any holiday, he could not abide to be alone, and Kate was not company enough.

He made expeditions, also, to gather copy for new work. Almost as soon as *Pickwick* was finished and while *Oliver Twist* was scarcely halfway through, he began work on *Nicholas Nickleby*, and with 'Phiz' travelled to Yorkshire to reconnoitre the notorious boarding schools there, on which Dotheboys Hall would be modelled. The Yorkshire schools were productive of maggots, fleas, beatings, and ignorance, but the fees were low, and where else could an illegitimate child be concealed by gentlefolk?

Travelling under assumed names, pretending to look for a school in which to place a young relative, Dickens and 'Phiz' were entertained along the way by a 'very queer old body' who turned out to be a mistress at one of the schools, returning from London with a letter to one of the boys from his father 'containing a severe lecture (enforced and aided by many texts from Scripture) *on his refusing to eat boiled meat*. She was very communicative, drank a great deal of brandy and water, and towards evening became insensible.' There was also 'a most delicious lady's maid' who begged them to watch out for the coach that would be sent to meet her. 'It is scarcely necessary to say that the Coach did not come, and a very dirty girl did.'

Right: 'The internal economy of Dotheboys Hall' – an illustration by Cruikshank for Nicholas Nickleby

They visited, among other schools, Bowes Academy, run by the one-eyed William Shaw. As a result of the beatings and putrescent food that he meted out, as many as ten of his pupils had been negligent enough to lose their sight. After paying damages, Shaw had been permitted to continue, losing on average one pupil a year by death. Suspicious of Dickens and 'Phiz', he made sure that they saw very little of his academy.

But Dickens's trained eye had seen enough in Yorkshire, and as soon as he was back in London he set to work on the new book, while continuing with his other commitments, to which he had added such marginal jobs as editing a book about the clown he had loved, Grimaldi. 'Mr Dickens writes too often and too fast' one reviewer remarked, echoing a widely felt astonishment at his prodigious industry. 'He has risen like a rocket, and', unless he eased up, 'will come down like the stick.' The remark nettled Dickens, but not so much as a plainly adverse reviewer, who said of *Oliver Twist* that 'What is good is not original, and what is original is not good.' Dickens was observed, after reading that, to stamp up and down the room, swearing, 'They shall eat their words.' He was distressed, too, by a stage adaptation of *Oliver Twist* – the defective copyright law permitted heedless piracies of any popular work, with no fee or respect to the author; this one was so excruciating that, after a few minutes, he lay down on the floor of the box and stayed there throughout. Of a pirated *Nicholas Nickleby*, however, he thought so well that he talked to its producer, Frederick Yates, about preparing a new dramatic version of *Oliver Twist* himself. It never happened. Dickens, instead, wrote a new farce for Macready, but it was so poor that Macready, with tact, rejected it.

Some months after the trip to Yorkshire, Dickens went north again, to see the dark satanic cotton-mills of Lancashire, and through the fog, grime and misery could discern 'no great difference' between the best and the worst of them. 'Disgusted and astonished', he vowed 'to strike the heaviest blow in my power for these unfortunate creatures', perhaps in *Nicholas Nickleby*, he thought, though in the event the blow was withheld until *Hard Times*. He did derive some material from the trip, modelling the Cheeryble brothers upon two merchants with whom he dined in Manchester.

Invitations were now being extended to him to enter the drawing rooms and salons of the highest society in London, the rich, cosmopolitan and cultured elite who circled around the mansions at the west end of town, as they had been doing since the Regency days when Byron and Shelley had been at their height. First, they assured themselves that Dickens would prove to be 'presentable'. When Bulwer-Lytton assured Lady Holland on that point, Dickens was invited to Holland House, a formidable experience. The liveried footman led guests up the grand Elizabethan staircase to be presented to a woman who looked like a falcon and had manners to suit. At dinner he might have listened to Macaulay discussing history, Samuel Rogers remembering Garrick, Boswell, Burke, and Madame de Staël, or the Reverend Sydney Smith minting witticisms that are still in currency. Very likely his hostess commanded him to pick up her fan, or draw the curtains. Dickens, as was his habit, took care not to speak much at such an occasion, and was in consequence rather admired as being 'very unobtrusive and altogether prepossessing', though his dress was considered intolerably dandified.

His natural inclination to dress up had been encouraged when he met the exquisite Count d'Orsay, another frequenter of Holland House and also, with his wife's stepmother, the witty and beautiful Countess of Blessington, the host of a glittering salon at Gore House. The elderly poet Walter Savage Landor, 'forty lions concentrated into one Poet' as Dickens described him, was one of the celebrities to be seen, Captain Marryat was another, and so were Wellington, Disraeli, Prince Louis Napoleon, and Lord Durham, whom posterity fondly recalls for his assurance that 'a man could jog along on forty thousand pounds a year'.

Samuel Rogers, a severely economical man, gave literary breakfasts at which the food was modest, but the guests were required to be lavish in their wit and learning, or Rogers's white head would fix them with his cold blue eyes, and an icy epigram deflate their morning spirits, among the old masters and rare editions. Sydney Smith approved of breakfast parties, on the grounds that, 'No one is conceited before one o'clock'.

It was a strictly mannered, often cruel world, but Dickens had already learned self-assurance, was a practised mimic of any tone, and felt confident in his intelligence and great gifts: gifts, he soon came to realize, that few of these privileged people had even a tiny part of. That awareness defended him against their insolence or patronization. He was acute enough to see behind the social masks, to see a kindness behind Lady Holland's beak, and a humanity in Rogers that expressed itself in friendliness to Kate on his visits to Doughty Street. Kate was never a guest at the great houses, for she had no mask, no wit.

Dickens must have searched his soul for signs of snobbishness in his enjoyment of it all; but he could not blame himself greatly for the keen amusement of knowing himself accepted at Holland House and Gore House fourteen years after he was accepted at Warren's blacking factory and the Marshalsea debtors' prison. He was, knowingly, indulging in what Lionel Trilling, apropos of Scott Fitzgerald, describes as 'the artist's frequent taste for aristocracy, his need – often quite open – of a superior social class with which he can make some fraction of common cause – enough, at any rate, to account for his own distinction.' When his novels are radically critical of the society he saw, the identified enemies are seldom the aristocratic, intellectual elite, but the masters of material gain and the parasites of materialism, in the law courts, the factories and workhouses. That, perhaps, is a limitation in him as a social critic, but it serves to defend him from the appearance of a hypocrite.

His political ideas were influenced by those of Thomas Carlyle, whose *History of the French Revolution* he carried in his pocket after meeting the author. Carlyle's expressed sympathy with the Chartist movement and his opinion that the unprivileged masses, the worst educated in Europe, had been utterly ignored in parliamentary reform, won Dickens's entire agreement.

It was at this time, also, that Dickens met Angela Burdett Coutts, the young heiress of two fortunes, which all her life she used, in her family tradition, to advance liberal schemes of social improvement. He quickly became her mentor and sounding-board, discussing slum clearance, homes for fallen women, Ragged Schools, and for many years advised her in confidence.

The Dickens's second child was born in March 1838 and named Mary. A month later, the first instalment of *Nicholas Nickleby* appeared, and Dickens rode into

Left: Baroness Angela Burdett-Coutts, with whom Dickens collaborated on many welfare schemes

town from Richmond, where he was staying briefly, to find out how it had done. The answer was staggering: on the first day it had sold nearly fifty thousand copies. At one o'clock that night Dickens and Forster rode out from London to Richmond exulting. *Oliver Twist*, too, continued to command a magnificent sale, and praise from most of the influential critics. Dickens had some wrangles with Cruikshank over the illustrations, but found Forster's advice valuable in the development and disposal of the characters. When he was about to finish the book, he for once declined Forster's invitation to go riding. The book demanded to be ended. He wrote to Forster, 'my missis is going out to dinner, and I ought to go, but I have a bad cold. So do you come, and sit here, and read, or work, or do something, while I write the LAST chapter of Oliver, which will be arter a lamb chop...and a bit o' som'at else.' Forster never forgot seeing Dickens write the last full stop and throw down his pen.

When Bentley brought out *Oliver Twist* in three-volume book form, it was the first to bear the name of Charles Dickens. There were few who did not already know the identity of Boz. But Bentley did not know Dickens well enough to retain him as an author and editor much longer. A running quarrel had grown up between them in which Bentley continually conceded ground, but without the graciousness that had preserved Chapman and Hall's association with Dickens. Each concession he wrung from Bentley only drove Dickens into a deeper dislike of the 'hound' and his unforgivable attitude. Dickens certainly exceeded his own contractual rights, and some observers of the dispute thought him simply dishonest. Macready wrote in his diary, 'He makes a contract which he considers advantageous at the time, but subsequently finding his talents more lucrative than he had supposed, he refuses to fulfil the contract.' Macready's observation was an exact one. The root of the quarrel was that when he first signed up with Bentley, Dickens was still only just entering the extraordinary success he now assuredly enjoyed. He could not have envisaged the sums of money his pen was capable of earning, nor the influential acquaintances he could now tap as an editor. On the other hand, whenever Bentley tried to enforce the initial agreements, he could be seen as a legalistic Shylock. An experienced publisher, he should have had more sympathy with this brilliant young man who was making money for both of them, and not have attempted to cash every last penny of what was due to his foresight in signing Dickens up so promptly.

The first dispute had concerned increases in Dickens's editorial salary as the monthly sales of *Bentley's Miscellany* increased, and the duration of the options Bentley had on his services. These points were settled by compromise, but there was a further issue at stake. Dickens had initially contracted with Bentley that, apart from a new novel for Chapman and Hall (which would be *Nicholas Nickleby*), his next two novels would belong to Bentley for £500 each: now Dickens wanted to regard *Oliver Twist* as one of those contracted novels, and to increase the

My dear Cruikshank.

I returned suddenly to town yesterday afternoon to look at the *eleven* ~~last~~ pages of Oliver Twist before it was delivered to the booksellers, when I saw the majority of the plates in the last volume for the first time.

With reference to the last one — Rose Maylie and Oliver. Without entering into the question of great haste or ~~without~~ any other cause which may have led to its being what it is — I am quite sure there can be little difference of opinion between us with ~~refer~~ respect to the result — May I ask you whether you will object to ~~doing~~ *designing* this plate afresh and doing so at once in order that as few impressions as possible of the present one may go forth?

I ~~take the liberty to tell~~ *feel confident* you know me too well to feel hurt by this enquiry, and with equal confidence in you I have lost no time in preferring it.

George Cruikshank

Left: A letter of complaint to George Cruikshank about one of the illustrations in Oliver Twist
Above: The offending illustration, now known as the 'fireside plate'

payment to £700, but Bentley insisted that, as it was appearing in instalments in the *Miscellany*, it represented Dickens's contribution as an editor, for which he had been paid already. Dickens answered that from the £700 Bentley might deduct the sums he had already paid on the instalments of *Oliver Twist*, that he wanted £600 for the second of the contracted works, and that in each case the payment would give Bentley the rights in only the first three thousand copies sold. Bentley agreed to give Dickens the money he asked for, but insisted on the entire copyrights and also another novel. Dickens answered by threatening to stop writing *Oliver Twist* altogether. Solicitors and arbitrators were now brought into the quarrel, but Bentley stopped short of going to court, for if he won, what use would a bitterly hostile editor be to his *Miscellany*? At last he yielded the point that *Oliver Twist* should be one of the two contracted novels.

Dickens, however, was still in full cry. This time it concerned the new number of the *Miscellany*, at the press: Bentley had been at the printers rearranging what Dickens had edited. 'I have been actually superseded in my office as Editor ... a gross insult.' He resigned from the post. Bentley, who had always had a friendly understanding with Dickens by which they informally shared the editorial judgements, replied that he was placing the matter in the hands of his solicitors and intended to hold Dickens to all his agreements. Dickens was obdurate, and said that no new instalment of *Oliver Twist* would be forthcoming.

Bentley yielded again, controlling his sullen mood in the hope (not one that was obviously ludicrous for a while yet) of retaining Dickens's valuable services. He conceded that his payments of £700 and £600 would buy him the rights only of the first three thousand copies of each novel, though after that he wished to share the income equally. As for the *Miscellany*, in the belief that Dickens's real complaint was a financial one, he offered to pay him forty guineas a month, back-dated to the very first issue.

Dickens was still not mollified. He wanted a clear demarcation between his duties and Bentley's on the *Miscellany*. A conference was arranged. Dickens was represented by Forster, whom Bentley had disliked as an 'ill-mannered man' on first sight, some months before. Throughout a long day a fresh agreement was hammered out, point after point being conceded to Dickens's interests. Dickens would agree to edit the *Miscellany* for the next three years, with a sliding scale of fees according to circulation. His duties and Bentley's were precisely defined. *Oliver Twist* would continue in the *Miscellany*, Bentley would pay a clear £500 for the book rights for three years, then the income would be shared. Similar terms, at £700, would apply to the second contracted novel, *Barnaby Rudge* (previously entitled *Gabriel Vardon*, and the source of friction with the late Macrone). Everything was straight now; Dickens had won most of the tactical engagements and their business went ahead: but both he and Bentley were still inwardly furious with the other.

Soon they were at it again. Bentley was introducing material into the *Miscellany* which Dickens thought unworthy of it. 'Order the *Miscellany* just as you please', he shrugged. 'I have no wish or care about the matter.' Then Bentley was making niggling deductions from Dickens's fees when his contributed pieces had to be trimmed to make room for others. Such small-mindedness, Dickens told him, made it impossible to 'wish for a very long continuance of our business connection'. Next it was *Barnaby Rudge*: Dickens could not possibly write it within the agreed time, he said, given that he was writing *Nicholas Nickleby* for Chapman and Hall, but why not instead introduce it as the new instalment work in the *Miscellany*? (It would be the same concession as Bentley had reluctantly made for *Oliver Twist*.) Bentley protested, but after six months (during which Dickens rashly took on more work for Chapman and Hall, a comic book, which in the event he could not produce) he once again capitulated. And still Dickens chafed. Alarmed by Bentley's advertising the 'forthwith' appearance of *Barnaby Rudge* when he had not even started writing it, he put it to Forster that he would like to be altogether free from the 'net' that Bentley had wound about him:

It is no fiction to say that at present I *cannot* write this tale. The immense profits which *Oliver* has realised to its publisher, and is still realising; the paltry, wretched, miserable sum it brought me . . . the consciousness that I have still the slavery and drudgery of another work on the same journeyman terms; the consciousness that my books are enriching everybody connected with them but myself, and that I, with such a popularity as I have acquired, am struggling in old toils, and wasting my energies in the very height and freshness of my fame, and the best part of my life, to fill the pockets of others, while for those who are nearest and dearest to me I can realise little more than a genteel subsistence: all this puts me out of heart and spirits: and I cannot – cannot and will not – under such circumstances that keep me down with an iron hand, distress myself by beginning this tale until I have had some time to breathe; and until the intervention of summer, and some cheerful days in the country, shall have restored me to a more genial and composed state of feeling.

Bentley agreed to postpone *Barnaby Rudge* for six months, on condition that Dickens did give himself 'time to breathe' by doing no work during that period except *Nicholas Nickleby*. A considerate concession, it only embarrassed Dickens, because Bentley did not know about the comic book he had taken on for Chapman and Hall. Dickens concealed his embarrassment behind an angry retort that he preferred to resign from the editorship of the *Miscellany*. Bentley learned about the comic book, but still contained his choler: he offered to pay £40 a month if Dickens would do no more than allow his name to continue to appear as editor and promise not to edit any other magazine. Dickens refused: Ainsworth must be appointed editor, he insisted, and then Dickens would announce his retirement with no acrimony, would offer Ainsworth his friendship and help, would make some contributions to the *Miscellany*, and have nothing to do with any other magazine for a year.

Bentley, seeing that Dickens would not budge and standing to gain little from taking him to court, agreed. There was still the matter of the book publication of *Barnaby Rudge*. After negotiations, it was agreed that Dickens should have a full year to write the book. He would, meanwhile, take on no fresh commitments. For the copyright, he would receive an initial £2000, with a further £2000 if sales reached fifteen thousand. In his triumph, Dickens indulged in a parting stab at the 'Burlington Street Brigand', remarking in his valedictory editorial that the magazine had 'always been literally "Bentley's" Miscellany, and never mine'.

When the full year was approaching its end, Dickens had written only two, chapters of *Barnaby Rudge*. He had been working hard at *Nicholas Nickleby*, but that was not the true explanation: rather, he was blocked by what had now turned into a detestation of Bentley. 'If I were a builder or a stone-mason I might fulfil my contract with him, but write for him I really cannot unless I am forced and have no outlet for escape.' He fabricated excuses, while Bentley insisted on the contract. Bentley advertised that *Barnaby Rudge* was forthcoming, Dickens advertised that it was not. Both prepared to go to court.

In the end, Bentley was advised that the legal position was not clear-cut and the case was certain to be expensive. He reconciled himself to losing Dickens. The agreed settlement was that Dickens paid Bentley £2250; in return Dickens had the sole copyright of *Oliver Twist*, possession of all the unsold copies of it and of Cruikshank's plates, and was released from the contract to deliver *Barnaby Rudge*.

The finance actually came from the ever-loyal Chapman and Hall, 'best of booksellers' as Dickens understandably entitled them. They paid him £3000 in consideration of a six-month copyright of *Barnaby Rudge*. Their terms for *Nicholas Nickleby* had been similar, except that the copyright term was five years and the deal also included a one-third share in the future profits of *Pickwick*.

The outcome of Dickens's long fight with Bentley was something more than figures and signatures on different bits of paper. The author's power of will, forged in the desperation of his earlier years and first tried on Macrone, had now been tested and tempered into a steel blade of determination, and blessed with victory. The 'Inimitable Boz' would henceforth be indomitable.

Chapter Ten

My Heart is at Windsor

JOHN DICKENS WAS NATURALLY PROUD OF HIS SON'S SUCCESS, and moreover grateful for it, since it served as security for his own improvidence, never mended. As soon as he had seen *Pickwick* rise, he trotted round to Chapman and Hall to touch them for a mere £4. Soon another passing difficulty obliged him to ask them for a little more help, the lack of which, he warned them, would be 'productive of fatal consequences'. They smiled and were touched, and soon were alarmed to hear that they alone once more stood between John Dickens and 'perdition'. And so it went on, until the tangle of bills and grandiloquence closed in, and less indulgent tradesmen than Chapman and Hall had him arrested for debt and served with an eviction order. 'Do the needful,' he asked the publishers. But his son it was who decided what was necessary, now that he heard the whole story for the first time, down to such details as his father's habit of snipping Charles's signatures from letters and selling them for a few shillings. It was intolerable for a man who had lately been elected a member of the Athenaeum, joining the club at the same time as Charles Darwin, to find that his father had been trading everywhere on his son's reputation.

Dickens took immediate and strict action. He paid off the most pressing creditors, then took the coach to Exeter, rented a small house in Alphington, furnished it, and packed his bewildered parents off there. After the first shock, in which they wrote him 'hateful, sneering letters', they found they quite liked it in Devon and stayed down there for four years. Dickens's solicitors, meanwhile, advertised in the press that he would not be responsible for debts incurred by 'certain persons having or purporting to have the surname of our said client'.

The summer of 1839 Dickens spent with his family in Petersham, across the river from Twickenham, and later at Broadstairs. The usual stream of visitors joined him in games of all sorts, indoor and outdoor, which he pursued with the exhausting ardour of his temperament. One such friend was the artist Daniel Maclise, who had been commissioned by Chapman and Hall to paint a portrait of Dickens. It turned out superbly well, and an engraving from it served as frontispiece to the three-volume edition of *Nicholas Nickleby*. The portrait itself was presented to Dickens at a lavish banquet.

Dickens told Forster that other publishers were making him attractive offers, but he was not inclined to leave Chapman and Hall. He had, however, a new project in mind which would require them to 'do something handsome, even handsomer perhaps than they dreamt of doing'. He wished to launch a weekly maga-

Opposite: Charles Dickens by Maclise. This portrait won high praise as a remarkable likeness when it was exhibited at the Royal Academy

86

zine. It would contain a miscellany of essays, tales, squibs at the law, character sketches, travel notes (Dickens might visit America, or Ireland), and the reborn Pickwick and Sam Weller. He would write the whole thing himself at the start, and if later on there were other contributors they would be chosen only by himself and paid what he said. As for himself, he would receive a salary, travelling expenses, and a share in the profits *before* expenses were deducted.

Chapman and Hall compliantly set about costing the project. Dickens secretly reassured himself about the figures they presented, having them independently confirmed by other printers. When a contract was drawn up, its provisions indicated that if the magazine sold fifty thousand copies weekly, as expected, Dickens would receive nearly £8000 a year in all; the publishers would receive rather less than half that sum, and would be liable to stand any losses that might occur. As a bonus, they gave him an extra £1500 for *Nicholas Nickleby*. It was not so much a contract as a testament to the steel blade of will that Dickens had perfected.

Next he turned to his domestic arrangements. Doughty Street no longer matched his success, his income, his admiration of the great houses he frequented. The family had been increased, also, by the birth of Kate Macready Dickens, his third child, on 29 October. He found what he was looking for near Regent's Park, 1 Devonshire Terrace, 'a house of great promise (and great premium), "undeniable" situation and excessive splendour'. He took a twelve-year lease, and set about improving the splendour. Deal doors were turned into mahogany, wooden mantels to marble, rugs to thick carpets, and the furniture of newly-weds to new, upholstered suites. The random assortment of books on the walls of his

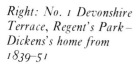

Right: No. 1 Devonshire Terrace, Regent's Park – Dickens's home from 1839–51

study made way for parades of great authors in fine bindings, to which rare volumes were periodically added.

Reviewing the arrangements of his life, Dickens could not stop short at reviewing his wife Kate; but as yet there were only hints – light flirtations with other women and condescensions to Kate – that their marriage was not as solid as the house they now inhabited. Kate was not amused when her husband took to wandering round the grand house singing

> My heart is at Windsor,
> My heart is not here,
> My heart is at Windsor
> A-following my dear.

The young fresh-faced Queen Victoria had just married Prince Albert, and Dickens, having watched the procession from the Athenaeum, for weeks after persisted in playing a charade of being desolate. That he had no taste, meanwhile, for doing any writing is a hint that, through the play-acting, he was working off some more serious perturbation. The charade went on beyond the point where his friends were tired of it, in letters like this to Forster:

I am utterly lost in misery and can do nothing.... The presence of my wife aggravates me. I loathe my parents. I detest my house. I begin to have thoughts of the Serpentine, of the Regent's Canal, of the razor upstairs, of the chemists down the street, of poisoning myself ... of hanging myself upon the pear-tree in the garden, of abstaining from food and starving myself to death ... of murdering Chapman and Hall and becoming great in story (SHE must hear something of me then – perhaps sign the warrant: or is that a fable?), of turning Chartist, of leading some bloody assault upon the palace and saving Her by my single hand.

In other letters, he professed to 'have fallen hopelessly in love with the Queen and wander up and down with vague dismal thoughts of running away to some uninhabited island with a maid of honour', preferably one who was 'beautiful and had no strong brothers'. Until they wearied of it, Forster and Maclise were persuaded to join in the heartsick game; Maclise was an object of Dickens's envy because he was in fact a favourite of the Queen's, and had been commissioned by her to paint secret pictures that she could give to Albert as presents. Through that connection, the two of them were able to prowl about Windsor Castle,

saw the corridor, and their private rooms, nay the very bed-chamber lighted up with such a ruddy, homely, brilliant glow bespeaking so much bliss and happiness that I, your humble servant, lay down in the mud at the top of the long walk and refused all comfort.... I have heard on the Lord Chamberlain's authority, that she reads my books, and is very fond of them. I think she will be sorry when I am gone. I should wish to be embalmed and to be kept (if practicable) on top of the triumphal arch at Buckingham Palace when she is in town, and on the northeast turret of the Round Tower when she is at Windsor.

Below: Queen Victoria and Prince Albert after their marriage on 10 February, 1840. Dickens's public professions that he had fallen 'hopelessly in love' with the young, fresh-faced Queen resulted in rumours that he was demented from overwork

Since Dickens indulged in the charade quite openly in public, it was not surprising that the newspapers reported rumours that he was demented by overwork: rumours that were started when Edwin Landseer joked that Dickens was 'raven mad', alluding to a mordant family pet to which Dickens was extravagantly devoted.

A year after Victoria's marriage, Dickens took a fancy to playing a similar game during a stay at Broadstairs. The objects of his affected ardour this time were two unmarried ladies, staying nearby, one of them of mature age, the other a young woman who had met Dickens once before and was fascinated and scared by him, particularly by the power of his luminous eyes. After many fantastic games with them, calling each in turn 'Queen of my heart', 'Beloved of my soul', 'Fair enslaver', issuing invitations to 'tread a measure with me, sweet lady' in a burlesque of stately dance, and being seized with poetic praise of their beauty, Dickens's mischief went further. One evening on the pier he caught the younger woman, Eleanor Picken, up in his arms, carried her to the brink of the rising tide, and swore they would stay there until the waves were over their heads. 'Let your mind dwell on the column in *The Times* wherein will be vividly described the fate of the lovely E.P. drowned by D. in a fit of dementia.' The sea was splashing them, and the girl struggled, shouting, 'O! my dress, my *best* dress, my *only* silk dress will be ruined.' When the water had reached her knees, she called out to Kate, 'Mrs Dickens, help me! Make Mr Dickens let me go.'

'Charles, how can you be so silly?' Kate called back. 'You'll spoil the poor girl's silk dress.'

'*Dress!*' Dickens shouted. 'Talk to me not of *dress*. When we already stand on the brink of the great mystery ... shall we be held back by the puerilities of silken raiment?'

Miss Picken extricated herself, and many years later published her account of that summer in Broadstairs, in which she observed that the whole of his family, including his parents, were subdued in Dickens's company, apparently nervous of him. She also recalls a visit she made to Devonshire Terrace some while later, when Dickens was cool to her, seeming to have forgotten the Broadstairs business. (He was probably irritated to have his work interrupted. A French admirer who once called at an inconvenient moment and sympathized with Dickens for having to put up with so many intruders, 'even madmen', was frogmarched out of the door by his host, who shouted, 'Yes, madmen, madmen! They alone amuse me.') Fred Dickens announced that he was off to see the murderer Courvoisier hanged. Dickens reproached him for his 'morbid craving to gloat over such a loathsome spectacle', then – though Miss Picken did not know about this – he decided that he ought to see a hanging for himself, just to confirm his doubts about it. The crowd had started to gather before midnight, and by the early morning were packed so tight that women fainted upright. The shouting and singing made an

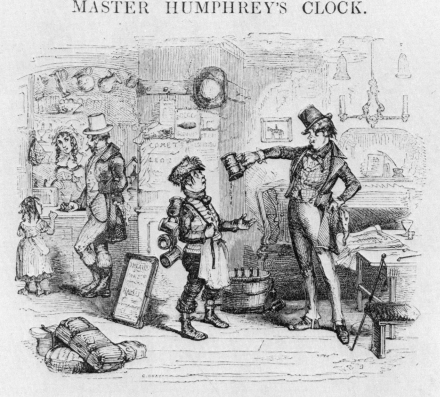

MASTER HUMPHREY'S CLOCK.

The Old Curiosity Shop.

CHAPTER THE THIRTY-EIGHTH.

IT—for it happens at this juncture, not only that we have breathing time to follow his fortunes, but that the necessities of these adventures so adapt themselves to our ease and inclination as to call upon us imperatively to pursue the track we most desire to take—Kit, while the matters treated of in the last fifteen chapters were yet in progress, was, as the reader may suppose, gradually familiarising himself more and more, with Mr. and Mrs. Garland, Mr. Abel, the pony, and Barbara, and gradually coming to consider them one and all as his particular private friends, and Abel Cottage Finchley as his own proper home.

Stay—the words are written, and may go, but if they convey any notion that Kit, in the plentiful board and comfortable lodging of his new abode, began to think slightingly of the poor fare and furniture of his old dwelling, they do their office badly and commit injustice. Who so mindful of those he left at home—

VOL. II.—27.   B

Left: An illustration by Phiz from The Old Curiosity Shop. *Serialized in* Master Humphrey's Clock *it pushed weekly sales to a hundred thousand copies*

Right: Nell's death as depicted by George Cattermole who collaborated with Browne on Barnaby Rudge *and* The Old Curiosity Shop

obscene festival of the execution, and Dickens was no less disgusted than he had expected.

The title of the new weekly magazine was *Master Humphrey's Clock*. Its first issue sold seventy thousand copies, and Dickens, hearing the news during a trip to Stratford-upon-Avon and Lichfield, was so exultant that he outspent the money he had with him and had to send Fred to a pawnbroker with their gold watches. 'What will the wiseacres say to weekly issues *now*?' he demanded, 'and what will they say to any of those ten thousand things we shall do together to make 'em writhe and stagger in their shoes. Thank God for this great hit. I always had a quiet confidence in it, but I never expected *this*, at first.' Nor, however, did he expect a desperate decline in sales as soon as the public, now used to meals from Dickens, realized that tit-bits were what the new weekly offered them. Less than a fortnight after the triumph of the first issue, there was a critical meeting at Chapman and Hall's offices. Dickens, always concerned about what his vast audience needed from him, at once came up with a proposal. He would expand a short story he had been planning for an early issue into a full-length serial novel, in spite of the difficulties of containing it within the brevity of weekly parts. It proved to be a master stroke: *The Old Curiosity Shop* so cemented the personal bond between author and readers that weekly sales rose to a hundred thousand.

The story of crowds on a New York pier shouting to a ship coming in from England 'Is Little Nell dead?' is familiar, but many comparable incidents testify to the serial's hold over readers high and low. As Little Nell's end approached, letters poured in to Dickens begging that she should not die. When she did, the Scottish critic Lord Jeffrey was found weeping in his library. 'I'm a great goose to have given way so', he sobbed, 'but I couldn't help it.' Macready, Landor, Thomas Carlyle and Edgar Allan Poe were all moved to a similar plight. So was Daniel O'Connell, reading on a train journey; he groaned, 'He should not have killed her', and threw the story out of the window – O'Connell, who had moved Dickens to tears in the House of Commons with his account of the misery of Ireland.

Dickens's own torment at the time has already been mentioned. A different torment attacked him in the course of writing *The Old Curiosity Shop*, facial rheumatism, brought on by the strain of writing in weekly episodes. The strain probably had something to do, also, with a painful row he had with his closest friend. Forster was in characteristic vein one night at Devonshire Terrace, 'one of his headlong streams of talk (which he thinks argument)' as Macready described it in his diary, and for once Dickens could not contain his exasperation with his friend's dogmatic arrogance. The argument turned to accusation, Forster becoming only more pompous. Dickens then pointed out that it was his house, and would Forster please leave it. Forster started to storm out, but was stayed by Macready, pleading that such a friendship should not be tossed away in one moment of temper. Dickens then offered his regret for having said what he had, but added that if Forster provoked him so again he would assuredly answer so. Forster did not want to walk out, nor did he feel able to stay without a better apology from Dickens, whose pride would not yield it. Forster stood there, hesitating, 'skimbling-skambling a parcel of unmeaning words', till he finally swallowed his anger and stayed on, though very silent for the rest of the evening.

More cheerful evenings were spent at the Clapham house of George Cattermole, who was one of the illustrators for *Master Humphrey's Clock*, 'Phiz' being the other. With the fondness that Victorian artists had for dining together and forming cliques, a group calling itself the Portwiners met regularly at Cattermole's and sat around a blazing fire, among carved furniture that had once been Byron's, drinking their port, smoking cigars, exchanging stories, opinions, and repartee. Apart from Dickens and Cattermole, there was Forster, Thackeray, Macready, Maclise, Bulwer-Lytton, the artists Charles and Edwin Landseer, and Mark Lemon, later editor of *Punch*.

Dickens could not relax his working schedule. No sooner had *The Old Curiosity Shop* been completed than *Barnaby Rudge* took its place in the demanding weekly parts of the *Clock*. The first episode appeared in February 1841, a few days after the birth of the Dickens's fourth child, a 'jolly boy' named Walter Landor Dickens.

Barnaby Rudge, the subject of so much contractual wrangling before a word was on paper, continued to give Dickens trouble. He told Forster, 'I didn't stir out yesterday, but sat and *thought* all day; not writing a line.' The struggle, it has been argued, arose from an ambiguity in Dickens himself. The most powerful pages in the book, two hundred of them, describe the Gordon Riots in London

in 1780. Dickens the successful author living in Devonshire Terrace, dining lavishly, dressing opulently, was attached to respectability and the rights of property and could not but be horrified by social violence; Dickens the man who had seen the squalor of Seven Dials, the misery of the Marshalsea, the flatulence of Parliament, felt a warm sympathy with the poor, and could understand those who would burst open the prisons and overthrow a society that violently protected privilege. He was in a double bind, no uncommon breeding-ground for an artist. When he was offered a seat in the Commons, as he was several times, he refused it: his books would be more effective instruments of reform, read, as they were, by people at all levels of society. But how could he confront that society with itself – its unemployment and poverty, its denial of education and suffrage, its starvation of men and women and maiming of small children in foundries and mines – how could he explain all that as the necessary result of the 'system', as he called it, yet deny men the right to seek a systematic change? A decade of strikes, of riots in Bristol, South Wales, Nottingham, Manchester, the North, had been brutally suppressed. What alternative, then, did men have but still more brutal measures against the system? Inevitably, Dickens was forced into the argument that Parliamentary reform was the only solution – reform, or rue. But his conscience could not flatly condemn men who were too desperate to wait patiently upon the reasoned improvements that the government of the richest nation in the world might see fit to allow itself.

In *Barnaby Rudge* he effectively sidestepped these questions by describing riots that had happened half a century earlier, and were ostensibly anti-Catholic, not anti-Parliament. That eighteenth-century order had passed, in society and in art. Of the Romantic movement, much nearer in time, there was enough in Dickens to give him a certain lurking taste for violent extremes.

Chapter Eleven

The Clock Stops

JUST SEVEN YEARS AFTER THE CUB REPORTER HAD WATCHED Earl Grey receive the freedom of Edinburgh, Dickens himself was granted the same honour, in June 1841. At the banquet he was greeted with cheers and a band playing 'Charley is My Darling'. Two hundred and seventy diners and nearly as many lady spectators saw him rise to acknowledge 'the kind opinion of the Northern people ... gladly and proudly'. Standing there, aged twenty-nine, among Scotland's most distinguished 'grey-headed men gathered about my brown flowing locks', he privately noticed his own calmness, 'cool as a cucumber'. As soon as he had arrived in Edinburgh, the city had risen to him. He had been 'introduced (I hope) to everybody in Edinburgh. The hotel is perfectly besieged, and I have been forced to take refuge in a sequestered apartment at the end of a long passage.' Throughout, an observer testified, 'he was a very fountain of mirth, bonhomie, and surprising anecdote'.

In his suite at the hotel, however, he had a room set aside 'for Clock purposes', and he continued to work at *Barnaby Rudge* throughout the fortnight in Edinburgh and a rainswept tour of the Highlands with Kate. Among the rocks and romantic glens, the ten-mile-long Glencoe made a 'terrible, awful, horrific' impression on them, he wrote to Forster. Swollen by rain,

... torrents were boiling and foaming, and sending up in every direction spray like the smoke of great fires. They were rushing down every hill and mountain side, and tearing like devils across the path, and down into the depths of the rocks. Some of the hills looked as if they had cracked in a hundred places. Others as if they were frightened, and had broken out in a deadly sweat. In others there was no compromise or division of streams but one great torrent came roaring down with a deafening noise, and a rushing of water that was quite appalling.

A frail, slippery footbridge took them across one gorge, but their carriage, fording the stream, found itself in a torrent so deep that the horses barely had their heads above the water.

It made me quite sick to think how I should have felt if Kate had been inside. The carriage went round and round like a great stone, the boy was as pale as death, the horses were struggling and plashing and snorting like sea-animals, and we were all roaring to the driver to throw himself off and let them and the coach go to the devil, when suddenly it all came right.

Back in England, by the more peaceable waters of Broadstairs, Dickens was

still humming with energy. He vied with his brother Fred in ludicrous commands
to the crew of a boat they went sailing in: with straight-faced authority they roared
out, 'Sheepshank your mizzen!' 'Abaft there, brail up your capstan-bar!' 'Now
then, a reef in your taffrail!' To a dogged admirer who followed him around,
Dickens finally remarked that he must be a native of the place, which the admirer
denied. 'Oh', Dickens said, 'I beg your pardon, I fancied I could detect Broad
Stares on your very face' – the sort of pun much enjoyed by all the Dickens family
and by the readers of *Punch*. Family and friends all surrounded the Dickenses
in those summer months.

*Left: The manuscript of
Barnaby Rudge*

The mornings were still dedicated to finishing *Barnaby Rudge*. Dickens's zest was increased by the prospect of a rest at last from writing when the story was completed. He argued himself into taking the rest by considerations of his market: to starve the readers of a new Dickens story for a year would greatly whet their appetite, whereas to continue uninterruptedly ran the risk of the fate that had befallen Walter Scott, who 'failed in the sale of his very best works, and never recovered his old circulation (though he wrote fifty times better than at first) *because he never left off*'.

Without question, the *Clock* must be stopped. Dickens was exhausted by a weekly deadline – it had made him so ill, indeed, that he had to undergo an operation for the removal of a fistula, the product of 'working overmuch', and took a month to recover. Besides, after the enormous success of *The Old Curiosity Shop*, the sales of the *Clock* that carried *Barnaby Rudge* had already dwindled to thirty thousand, and would dwindle faster if he was not writing it. Chapman and Hall agreed to revert to publishing a new work in monthly parts; but when Forster, acting for Dickens, proposed that it could wait for a year, serving to 'put the town in a blaze again' when it was produced, the publishers were left speechless. However, 'the best of booksellers' took the point, and settled upon terms even more

Right: A painting of Dolly Varden (Barnaby Rudge) *by W. P. Frith*

Opposite: The earliest known photograph of Dickens from a daguerreotype by Unbek made at the time of his visit to America in 1843

lucrative to Dickens than hitherto, including £150 a month during the year's rest.

At once Dickens asked himself what he could do with the the interval, and irresistibly the answer came to him – visit the United States. Vague thoughts of it had been in his mind for some time, and the American writer Washington Irving, in the course of admiring letters dating from the time of *The Old Curiosity Shop*, had promised 'it would be a triumph for me from one end of the States to the other, as was never known in any nation', not even in Edinburgh. The project was a 'haunting' one not simply for that reason; the United States represented a political scheme of things that had solved and transcended the questions he had faced, painfully, in *Barnaby Rudge*. There, he believed, the syndrome of privilege and poverty had been broken by the democratic ideals of a young nation. He wanted to see it all for himself while he was young, witness and bear witness, and expose English detractors of the United States as prejudiced and short-sighted. 'Why cannot you go down to Bristol', Lady Holland asked him, 'and see some of the third- and fourth-class people there and they'll do just as well?"

Kate hated the project on better grounds. How could they possibly make so arduous a journey with three small children and a baby? Dickens, having taken advice from Macready, decided that the answer was to leave the children behind: first Fred, then Macready, would look after them. Kate's tears ran hotter: she could not bear to be separated from her children for six months. It was her duty to accompany her husband, Macready told her, and to be happy in doing it. Not happily, but resignedly, Kate submitted, and preparations were put in hand. Dickens was restless to be off.

He spent weeks excitedly planning the journey, sitting among piles of travel books and maps, with Macready, who had been to North America, and Forster to advise him. He had met some American visitors in London on whom he might call, and there was no shortage of letters of introduction to many distinguished American citizens. There were whole wardrobes of elegant clothes to be ordered for Kate and himself, and the Devonshire Terrace house had to be let for their absence. Chapman and Hall were to arrange the passages.

They kissed their children goodbye on 2 January 1842, and, accompanied by Forster and a maid for Kate, travelled to Liverpool. The ship was the *Britannia*, which two years earlier had been commissioned as the first steamship on a regular mail service across the Atlantic. Their cabin was so hilariously tiny that their port-manteaux could 'no more be got in at the door ... than a giraffe could be forced or persuaded into a flowerpot'.

Two days later, above a muddle of rigging and trunks, stewards and farewell tears, the great red funnel poured out its black smoke and the ship carried them out into the fog of the Atlantic.

Chapter Twelve

National Vanity

THE SEA TRIP WAS WORSE EVEN THAN KATE HAD IMAGINED, THE roughest passage for years. Everything on the ship, including the passengers, rolled around distractedly for a fortnight. Dickens, himself sick, did what he could for Kate and Anne, her maid, making up pills from their medicine chest while the tiny scales rocked, and serenading them with an accordion he borrowed. The gales grew so violent that the funnel had to be lashed down. The lifeboats were smashed, so was the wooden casing of the paddle-wheels. Two days off Halifax the sea subsided, but Kate's conviction of doom was reinforced when an incompetent pilot steered the ship aground on a mudbank. The passengers and many of the crew rushed on deck in panic as the breakers crashed around them, and distress rockets were fired into the night sky. Captain Hewett remained calm, and the ship scraped into a lagoon from which they could sail on at high tide.

The next morning they were gliding past the clapboard houses and cheering crowds of Halifax, Nova Scotia. No sooner had the ship tied up than Dickens was ashore, arm-in-arm with the ship's doctor, looking for oysters. But the 'triumph' that Washington Irving had promised him commenced on the instant. The Speaker of the House of Assembly rushed up, breathless, and insisted that Dickens accompany him; Kate, still recovering from the voyage, would be fetched later.

Then [Dickens wrote to Forster] he drags me up to the Governor's house, and then Heaven knows where; concluding with both houses of Parliament. I wish you could have seen the crowds cheering the Inimitable in the streets. I wish you could have seen judges, law-officers, bishops and law-makers welcoming the Inimitable. I wish you could have seen the Inimitable shown to a great elbow-chair by the Speaker's throne ... listening with exemplary gravity to the queerest speaking possible, and breaking in spite of himself into a smile as he thought of this commencement to the Thousand and One stories in reserve for home.

Arriving at Boston two days later, Dickens was met by a dozen reporters who leapt on board before the ship had moored and wrung him by the hand. What the Americans saw was a smallish man, in what they described as 'full-fig': under a fur greatcoat he wore a brown frock-coat, a waistcoat figured in red and adorned by a gold watch-chain, and an extravagant cravat fastened by two linked diamond pins. His flowing brown ringlets were surmounted by a beaver hat. The ornateness did not surprise those who had seen engravings of Maclise's *Nickleby* portrait; what did strike them was the youthful, animated sensitivity of the face. 'He seemed all on fire with curiosity, and alive as I never saw mortal before', one wrote. 'He seemed like the Emperor of Cheerfulness on a cruise of pleasure, determined to conquer a realm or two of fun every hour.'

Before Dickens had even set foot on land, the invitations had started to pour in, the requests for autographs, the gifts and demands. On his first night in Boston he was free, after dinner, to stretch his voyage-weary legs by running delightedly through the tidy, historic streets of Boston, over the snow, in the company of a friend from the voyage, the Earl of Mulgrave. He was seldom to enjoy such freedom again in the vastness of the continent. Everywhere he went the crowds pressed at him, cheering, staring, wringing his hand, clipping fur from his coat, adulating him as pop stars are a century later. At the theatre he had to bow in

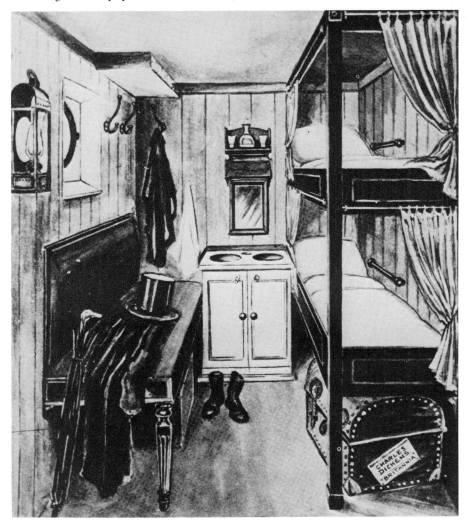

Left: Dickens's state-room on the Britannia

acknowledgement of specially composed Boz Waltzes: at the Boz Ball the fantastically elaborate decorations celebrated the characters of his novels. Two artists attended him, one sketching for a portrait, the other measuring his physiognomy with calipers for a bust, while Dickens, eating his breakfast, autographed cards prepared for him by the secretary he had had to engage, George Putnam. When he travelled, heads were thrust in at the carriage window to gaze at him. More than once, he had to resort to locking himself in a room while the crowds thronged outside the door.

At first he enjoyed it all thoroughly, noting his own calm, as he had in Edinburgh. 'There never was a king or emperor upon the earth so cheered and followed by crowds, and entertained in public at splendid balls and dinners', he wrote. 'Authorities from nearly all the states have written to me. I have heard from the universities, congress, senate, and bodies, public and private, of every sort and kind.' He was introduced to leading citizens and prominent artists and intellectuals, and met thousands of other guests at daily receptions. 'It is no nonsense, and no common feeling', he was assured by Dr Channing, the Unitarian. 'It is all heart.'

The republican vision was confirmed by the tours of institutions that Dickens undertook in Boston, and would repeat wherever he went. The school for blind, deaf and dumb children, the hospital for the insane, the orphanage, the reform school, the prison, the broad-minded universities, and best of all the industrial mills of Lowell, where the working girls enjoyed many advanced ideas of welfare – all of them were eloquent of the supremacy of a democratic nation over privilege-bound England. 'There is no man in this town, or in this State of New England, who has not a blazing fire and a meat dinner every day of his life. A flaming sword in the air would not attract so much attention as a beggar in the streets.' The people he found good-natured, frank, and hospitable: subscriptions were raised to meet his hotel bills, but he politely insisted on paying them from his own pocket.

But as the lionizing grew ever more demanding and intrusive, he began to detect more hysteria than heart in it.

I can do nothing that I want to do [he complained in a letter to Forster], go nowhere where I want to go, and see nothing that I want to see. If I turn into the street, I am followed by a multitude. If I stay at home, the house becomes, with callers, like a fair. If I visit a public institution, with only one friend, the directors come down incontinently, waylay me in the yard, and address me in a long speech. I go to a party in the evening, and am so enclosed and hedged about by people, stand where I will, that I am exhausted for want of air. I go to church for quiet, and there is a violent rush to the neighbourhood of the pew I sit in, and the clergyman preaches at *me*. I take my seat in a railroad car, and the very conductor won't leave me alone. I get out at a station, and can't drink a glass of water, without having a hundred people looking down my throat when I open my mouth to swallow.... By every post, letters on letters arrive, all about nothing, and all demanding an immediate answer. This man is offended because I won't live in his

house; and that man is disgusted because I won't go out more than four times in one evening. I have no peace, and am in a perpetual worry.

He began to make excuses to cancel engagements. One hostess, having prepared a superlative dinner for the Dickenses, received their apologies half an hour after it was finished. Among the staid Bostonians, remarks were made about Dickens's manners, how he had combed his hair at the dinner table, made indiscreet comments on women of his London acquaintance, was too flashy a dresser.

What really stirred up feeling, however, was his speech at the climax of his Boston visit, a banquet in his honour. The guests, who had paid £3 a ticket, first heard Josiah Quincy pay homage to the social reformer, the fighter for the downtrodden. 'He infuses a moral tone into everything. He is not only a portrayer of public wrongs, but he makes men feel that there is no condition so degraded as not to be visited by gleams of a higher nature.' This was the portrait of Dickens that the Americans had, and they wanted him to match it.

In answer, he was glad to fulfil their expectations at first, but then moved on to another subject, the question of international copyright. There was no law (nor would there be for fifty years) to restrain piracy of a writer's work abroad without a penny to the author. Dickens knew himself to be 'the greatest loser by it', but he was moved by more than self-interest. His blood boiled, he wrote to Forster, when he thought of Walter Scott crushed by debt, while millions in the United States devoured his work. Copyright protection, he told the Boston dinner, was of equal importance to the advancement of American literature. 'The affectionate regard of my fellow men' mattered far more than money, but affection and justice were not incompatible. He sat down to great applause, but no subsequent speaker referred to copyright law.

The newspapers the next morning bayed at him, at his gross insult to those who wished to honour him and were instead lectured about his income; which was strange, since the same newspapers were the most eager pirates of his and other authors' work, often rehashing it to suit their own tastes. Nevertheless, it was a controversy that remained on heat for the rest of Dickens's time in America, and beyond it.

Dickens was dismayed that American men of letters dared not support him in public. They were amazed by his audacity at raising what they all agreed, privately, was 'an enormous fraud'. Only a few of the more respectable journals spoke out in his defence. Deliberately he advanced the argument again when he spoke in Hartford, and was advised by the newspaper next morning, 'It happens that we want no advice on the subject.' As always, in the face of opposition Dickens became 'iron upon this theme', and determined not to let it drop. He asked Forster to procure from the leading authors in England a joint letter in his support, which he would have published in the best journals. The reaction to his speeches, he told Forster sorrowfully, had fundamentally upset his belief in American freedom

Left: The Extra Boz Herald *described the 'Boz Ball' held in Dickens's honour in New York, 14 February 1842*

THE EXTRA BOZ HERALD.

NEW YORK, TUESDAY MORNING, FEBRUARY 15, 1842.

PORTRAIT OF DICKENS.

Boz.

The Ball

Mrs. Leo Hunter's Dress Déjeûné

Ramble and Mrs. Corney Taking Tea

Nicholas Teaching French to the Kenwigs

Quilp Fighting the Scaffold Figure

The Middle-aged Lady in the Double-bedded Room

Mr. and Mrs. Mantalini in Ralph Nickleby's Office

Mrs. Bardell faints in Mr. Pickwick's arms

Oliver Twist at Mr. Maylie's Door

Mrs. Bardell Encounters Mr. Pickwick in the Prison

Little Nell and her Grandfather, the Mild ——— picked Apprentice

The Seduced Mrs. Dombey

The Stranger Soliloquising Beautifully in Front of Mr. Winkle's Cottage

The Stranger Witchery Playing in the Cottage

The Pickwick Club.

Washington Irving in England and Charles Dickens in America

of speech in matters of controversy. 'I do fear', he wrote, 'that the heaviest blow ever dealt at liberty will be dealt by this country, in the failure of its example to the earth.' What he had taken to be blemishes upon American democracy now began to seem like the substance of the country (although it was in Hartford that he was delighted to be greeted by an assembly of car-men, all in their blue overalls, and all familiar with his work).

In New York Cornelius Mathews did speak up, at the Dickens Dinner, in support of copyright law. He was ignored by the press, with one exception, the *Tribune*, in which the embattled Horace Greeley urged Dickens not to be deterred from spelling out justice by any 'mistaken courtesy' to publishers and readers who had profited from piracy and now offered him only 'acres of inflated compliments soaked in hogsheads of champagne'. Not that Dickens, of all people, needed advice to be determined: but such cordial sentiments heartened him, as did a petition for an international copyright law on which, eventually, the signatures of many leading writers followed Washington Irving's.

Irving's humour, when the two men met in New York, Dickens found a delight. He was captivated, too, by Mrs David Cadwallader Colden, the sister-in-law of Lord Jeffrey and wife of an actor admired by Macready. He wrote her flirtatious letters for years afterwards. In Boston he had found a warm friend in Cornelius Felton, the oyster-loving Harvard Professor of Greek, and another in the poet Longfellow, whom he conducted round the slums of London one night later in 1842, when Longfellow visited him.

The slums of New York, fermenting with sleeping heaps of negro women the night Dickens visited them, could learn nothing from London's in depravity and

Right: A ticket for the 'Boz Ball'

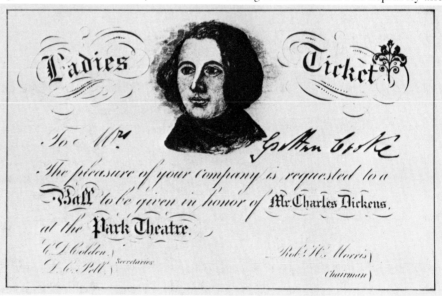

dereliction. Nor were the city's public institutions the slightest bit as impressive as those he had seen in Boston; the rat-run, crammed Tombs prison was particularly disgusting.

Apart from the Dickens Dinner and the Boz Ball, Dickens refused to participate in any other public spectacles of himself in New York. After three weeks his party left the City and headed for the South and the Mid-West, where he hoped to be more a 'free agent'.

That hope was quickly dashed in Philadelphia. Dickens agreed to meet a few gentlemen of that city. At once it was advertised in the newspaper that he would be 'gratified to shake hands with his friends', and six hundred people collected outside the hotel. The landlord told him there would be mayhem if he refused to meet them, so he did, shaking hands for two hours. Subsequently the landlord overcharged him for his stay at the hotel, a not infrequent incident, though there were also hoteliers who were reluctant to accept any payment at all. There was one man in Philadelphia whom Dickens was glad to meet, Edgar Allan Poe.

In Washington he saw Congress in session and, as at Westminster, was disenchanted by the mediocrity that prevailed over the few 'noble' men, notably John Quincey Adams. A hilarious audience with President Tyler has been described by Edgar Johnson:

The President rose, and said, 'Is *this* Mr Dickens?' 'Sir, it is.' 'I am astonished to see so young a man, Sir', said the President. Dickens smiled, and thought of returning the compliment, but the President looked so worn and jaded 'that it stuck in my throat like Macbeth's amen'. 'I am happy to join with my fellow citizens, warmly, in welcoming you to this country', said the President. The two men shook hands. Then they sat and looked at each other until Dickens rose, observing that doubtless the President's time was fully occupied and that he had better go.

Beside him, the President had a spit box. In the lobby outside his office, people waiting to see him all chewed 'mighty quids of tobacco.... They all constantly squirted forth upon the carpet a yellow saliva which quite altered its pattern.'

In the courts of law, the judge has his spittoon on the bench, the counsel have theirs, the witness has his, the Prisoner his, and the crier his. The jury are accommodated at the rate of three men to a spittoon.... I have twice seen gentlemen at evening parties in New York, turn aside when they were not engaged in conversation, and spit upon the drawing-room carpet. And in every bar-room and hotel passage the stone floor looks as if it were paved with open oysters.

Worse yet, when they were travelling 'the flashes of saliva flew so perpetually and incessantly out of the windows all the way' that Dickens was obliged to lay his fur coat down and 'wipe the half-dried flakes of spittle from it with my handkerchief'. Travelling on a stage coach, Kate was sprayed all night by a smartly dressed co-traveller.

In spite of such trials and a recurrent infection, Kate proved herself 'a most admirable traveller' in her husband's eyes; she 'has pleased me very much, and proved herself perfectly game'. She had a propensity to clumsiness, constantly bruising herself and dropping things, but she had borne up against a wretched

homesickness. Wherever they stayed, she set up a watercolour portrait of the children that Maclise had painted for them as a going-away present: but because of continued gales in the Atlantic, no letters from England reached them until they were in Washington. The packet arrived while Dickens was at a dinner: Kate nobly did not start to read the news until he was there to share in the joy. On an accordion he had bought, Dickens tenderly played her 'Home, Sweet Home' every night.

From Washington they went on to Virginia, where the sight of slavery and white attitudes to it revolted Dickens's deepest feelings. He saw white poverty, too, in southern Pennsylvania, wretched broken-down homesteads and a landscape desolated by clearance. Travelling by riverboat to St Louis, the farthest point west of their journey, he detested the slimy Mississippi, and was critical of the minimal toilette that American travellers allowed themselves. Once when he was washing himself in his cabin, and Kate lay in bed, 'a party of "gentlemen" ' stared in at the window, transfixed. He kept himself fit by jogging along for miles beside the coaches they rode in, but 'the greater part of the men will sit and shiver round the stove all day rather than put one foot before another. As to having a window open, that's not to be thought of' – every hotel room and rail carriage was intolerably over-heated. He became convinced that the United States contained a majority of the world's 'intensified bores'. A party in Cincinnati included 'at least one hundred and fifty first-rate bores.... I really think my face has acquired a fixed expression of sadness from the constant and unmitigated boring I endure.' His boredom may have been an index of his own homesickness, or perhaps, it has been suggested, he simply could not pick up the dry humour of Americans.

The merriest day they had was a journey from Columbus to Sandusky in a privately hired four-horse coach, along a 'cord' road surfaced with logs laid crosswise – like 'going up a steep flight of stairs in an omnibus', Dickens said. They were thrown and banged around for hours, but 'the day was beautiful, the air delicious, and we were *alone*, with no tobacco spittle, or eternal prosy-conversation about dollars and politics (the only two subjects they ever converse about, or can converse about) to bore us. We really enjoyed it.' They had a picnic in the forest, drinking 'to our darlings and all friends at home', ran through a lightning storm, and finally reached Sandusky very late. Putnam, driven from his room by bedbugs, slept in the coach, where he was besieged by pigs who, 'looking upon the coach as a kind of pie with some manner of meat inside, grunted round it so hideously that he was afraid to come out again, and lay there shivering, til morning'.

Putnam, in fact, was unwittingly a perennial amusement as well as being an indefatigable secretary and general manager. He was keen to sing to the Dickenses, asking if, in their fatigue, they didn't feel the need of 'a little soothing' from his voice. He admired Dickens's high spirits throughout all the anxieties of the journey, and noted how, when his employer was writing letters home, his face 'would be convulsed with laughter at his own fun'. Their other companion, the maid Anne, was an indispensable comfort to Kate and managed the journey very well, chiefly by a wholly English refusal to be impressed by anything. At the Niagara Falls, where Dickens felt an awe as at a 'tremendous ghost' (and wished Mary had been there to see it), Anne observed 'nothing but water'. The only emotion she showed in five months was a conviction that they would be scalped by Indians.

From Niagara they went into Canada, and Dickens felt more at home among British reserve. In Montreal he met Lord Mulgrave again, and together they staged a theatrical evening at the Coldstream Guards' garrison, where Mulgrave was the Commander's aide-de-camp. Dickens directed and managed the show with a comprehensive attention to every detail that was typical of him at all times, and especially witnessed to his enthusiasm for theatre. He played several parts himself. Kate too went on stage, and astonished him by playing 'devilish well'.

He kept up his theatrical antics and roaring spirits when they were on the Atlantic again, having embarked from New York on 7 June. The three-week voyage home was in complete contrast to the outward one, on a sailing packet across a benign ocean, with two staterooms for accommodation.

They arrived at Devonshire Terrace after the children's bedtime, but it was not long before the family was ecstatically reunited. Five-year-old Charley had a seizure, having, as he remarked, got 'too glad'. In games and songs with the children, heartfelt greetings of old friends, a holiday at Broadstairs, a trip with Forster, Maclise and Clarkson Stanfield to the Arthurian haunts of Cornwall – 'I never laughed in my life, as I did on this journey' – Dickens exulted in being home again. Soon he was planning a new novel. But first there was his volume of *American Notes*, that he had finished in four months.

His real disappointment in the country he had poured out, while still in the United States, to Macready. 'This is not the republic I came to see; this is not the republic of my imagination', he wrote.

The more I think of its youth and strength, the poorer and more trifling in a thousand aspects it appears in my eyes. In everything of which it has made a boast – excepting its education of the people and its care for poor children – it sinks immeasurably below the level I had placed it upon; and England, even England, bad and faulty as the old land is, and miserable as millions of her people are, rises in comparison.

In their 'national vanity', he believed, 'Americans can't bear to be told of their faults'. Now he told them of some of them in *American Notes*, but with a courteousness and tact that suppressed the journalist and reformer in him. Amid much praise for the people, he attacked slavery, the 'smart man' business ethos, and the filthy yellow press, which bore much responsibility for the very low 'average of general information' among the Americans. Of the outcry over international copyright he wrote not a word, though while he had still been in the United States

Private Theatricals.

COMMITTEE,

Mrs. TORRENS,
W. C. ERMATINGER, Esq.

Mrs. PERRY.
Captain TORRENS.

THE EARL OF MULGRAVE.

STAGE MANAGER—MR. CHARLES DICKENS.

QUEEN'S THEATRE, MONTREAL,

ON WEDNESDAY EVENING, MAY 25TH, 1842,

WILL BE PERFORMED,

A ROLAND FOR AN OLIVER.

MRS. SELBORNE.	*Mrs Torrens*
MARIA DARLINGTON.	*Miss Griffin*
MRS. FIXTURE.	*Miss Ermatinger*
MR. SELBORNE.	*Lord Mulgrave*
ALFRED HIGHFLYER.	*Mr Charles Dickens*
SIR MARK CHASE.	*Honorable Mr Methuen*
FIXTURE.	*Captain Willoughby*
GAMEKEEPER.	*Captain Granville*

AFTER WHICH, AN INTERLUDE IN ONE SCENE, (FROM THE FRENCH,) CALLED

Past Two O'clock in the Morning.

THE STRANGER.	*Captain Granville*
MR. SNOBBINGTON.	*Mr Charles Dickens*

TO CONCLUDE WITH THE FARCE, IN ONE ACT, ENTITLED

DEAF AS A POST.

MRS. PLUMPLEY.	*Mrs Torrens*
AMY TEMPLETON.	*Mrs Charles Dickens* !!!!!!! ....
SOPHY WALTON.	*Mrs Perry*
SALLY MAGGS.	*Miss Griffin*
CAPTAIN TEMPLETON.	*Captain Torrens*
MR. WALTON.	*Captain Willoughby*
TRISTRAM SAPPY.	*Doctor Griffin*
CRUPPER.	*Lord Mulgrave*
GALLOP.	*Mr Charles Dickens*

MONTREAL, May 24, 1842.

GAZETTE OFFICE.

Left: A playbill for a production Dickens staged in Montreal in 1842. The actors names have been written in by Dickens and they include his wife in the part of Amy Templeton in Deaf as a Post

113

the Boston publishing interests had successfully lobbied Congress to disregard his argument.

The book's reception in the American yellow press can be imagined. Already, shortly after his return to England, the New York papers had given currency to a spurious letter in which Dickens was supposed to have expressed himself disobligingly about the 'uncouth' treatment he had experienced in America, and the letter was widely taken to be authentic. Now, confronted with the polite disappointment of *American Notes* (which was pirated in scores of thousands of copies, taken from stolen proof sheets, before the English editions arrived), the American papers could not find enough adjectives – coarse, vulgar, impudent, superficial, narrow-minded, conceited cockney, flimsy, childish, trashy, contemptible, were among the first flowering – to describe the man who had dared to write about 'this original and remarkable country'. It is true, of course, that in five crowded months Dickens could not have acquired more than a slight knowledge of the country, which he exaggerated into generalizations, but among his American friends, such as Longfellow and Felton, it was felt to be 'a capital book; lively, spirited, true and good-humoured'. English opinions of the book were, on the whole, cool, but it brought him in £1000 towards the cost of the journey.

Chapter Thirteen

Such Dinings

THE NEW NOVEL THAT DICKENS WOULD WRITE AFTER A YEAR'S rest from fiction was *Martin Chuzzlewit*. To make a beginning he found more difficult than ever, perhaps because the year off had swamped his reservoir of ideas, or made him self-conscious: it was to be the first of his novels in which everything depends upon a single theme, selfishness. 'Dejected', 'sullen', 'horribly cross', he paced his room for days before he could put a sentence on paper. Once he had got going, however, he was sure that it was 'immeasurably' the best book he had written so far. The public did not agree: sales were down to twenty thousand a month, a fifth of the figure that *The Old Curiosity Shop* had attained weekly. To stir up the sluggish audience, Dickens decided that he would send young Martin Chuzzlewit off to the United States, and did so in the sixth instalment.

That sort of decision in a novelist sounds like an arbitrary one to us nowadays, although it is a familiar device in a television series. (How Dickens would have relished writing for television!) But Dickens never scorned the demands and tastes of his audience, and it was possible for him to respond on the wing by virtue of the improvization that writing in instalments allowed him, a form that he always preferred in spite of the sniffs of authors who thought it vulgar. Not that he was in the least degree an 'inspirational' writer. Perhaps there was something of that in *Pickwick*, which he wrote with the zest of a new author, and one, moreover, who was concurrently doing several other literary jobs. But his publisher, Frederick Chapman, testified to the very careful sketching and plotting that Dickens put into his later books and the extensive rewriting that he did at both manuscript and proof stages. As for the actual process of invention, Dickens's daughter Mary remembered how, when she was a girl, she had had a long illness and during her convalescence had been granted the rare privilege of lying in her father's study while he worked.

Although I was fearful of disturbing him, he assured me that he desired to have me with him. On one of these mornings I was lying on the sofa endeavouring to keep perfectly quiet, while my father wrote busily and rapidly at his desk; when he suddenly jumped from his chair and rushed to a mirror which hung near, and in which I could see the reflection of some extraordinary facial contortions which he was making. He returned rapidly to his desk, wrote furiously for a few minutes, and then went to the mirror. The facial pantomime was resumed, and then turning inwards, but evidently not seeing me, he began talking rapidly in a low voice. Ceasing this soon, however, he returned once more to his desk, where he remained silently writing until luncheon-time.

116

Left: 'Mr Pecksniff announces himself as the shield of Virtue'. A scene from Martin Chuzzlewit *drawn by Phiz*

It was a curious experience for me, and one of which I did not until later years fully appreciate the purport. Then I knew that with his natural intensity he had thrown himself completely into the character that he was creating, and that for the time being he had not only lost sight of his surroundings, but had actually become in action, as in imagination, the personality of his pen.

After a morning's close work he was sometimes quite preoccupied when he came into luncheon. Often ... he would come in, take something to eat in a mechanical way, and return to his study to finish the work he had left, scarcely having spoken a word. Our talking at these times did not seem to disturb him, though any sudden sound, as the dropping of a spoon or the clinking of a glass, would send a spasm of pain across his face.

117

Right: '*Mrs Gamp
proposes a Toast*'. *A Phiz
illustration for* Martin
Chuzzlewit

Except when he was terribly laden with work, in his maturity Dickens wrote at regular hours, chiefly in the mornings. He was methodical and disciplined with himself, always rearranging the desk and the furniture of his workroom, wherever he stayed, to suit the order he was used to. He was punctilious in his personal appearance, and demanded an equal orderliness from the rest of his family, making a daily inspection of the children's rooms with what Henry James called his 'military eye', and reprehending the slightest untidiness by means of a note, neatly folded and pinned to a pin-cushion. The domestic arrangements and timetable of the household had to be just so.

118

In the wicked burlesque of the American scenes in *Martin Chuzzlewit*, Dickens worked off his impatience with that country which he had politely restrained in *American Notes*. The abuse with which that restraint had been rewarded in the United States worked the familiar mechanism in Dickens: 'I have a strong spice of the Devil in me; and when I am assailed, as I think falsely or unjustly, my red hot anger carries me through it bravely.' When *Martin Chuzzlewit* was read in the United States the response to it was naturally an insensate rage. On stage, a copy of the book was added to the ingredients that the witches in *Macbeth* toss into their cauldron. They were 'all stark staring raving mad across the water', Dickens remarked, and when Macready was about to sail to America he refused to accompany him even to Liverpool, for fear that Americans, seeing Macready in friendship with Dickens, would pour down upon the actor's head 'every species of insult and outrage'.

In burlesque, as in polite observations, Dickens remained only a witness of the United States. For England, in *Martin Chuzzlewit*, his humour had the insider's bitterness, until the later chapters. The inexhaustible Mrs Gamp is a brutalized victim of the society in which Mr Pecksniff's greased hypocrisy rules. The harshness, comic but ungenial, was new to Dickens's readers, who, in spite of enjoying the American scenes, still remained few in comparison to previous audiences. It was a disappointment to Dickens, of course, but also to his publishers, who wondered if they had been unwise to consent to his year's absence from the readers.

One day in the Strand offices William Hall committed one of the tiny errors that alter a life. Thinking aloud rather than advancing the proposition to Dickens, he referred to a clause in their contract by which, in the event of lower sales than anticipated, the author's monthly salary might be reduced from £200 to £150. Dickens reacted as Lady Holland would have to an insolent footman, or as he would have liked to react himself when Maria Beadnell had called him a 'boy'. To be fair, it was from Dickens, of course, that Chapman and Hall had derived all the prosperity they now enjoyed; but it is most unlikely that they would have rigidly enforced the clause.

The mere thought was far too much for Dickens. 'I am so irritated', he told Forster, 'so rubbed in the tenderest part of my eyelids with bay-salt, by what I told you yesterday that a wrong kind of fire is burning in my head, and I don't think I *can* write ... I am bent upon paying Chapman and Hall *down*.' Forster advised him to let his temper cool down before taking any action, but Dickens, always ignited by injustice to anybody, was unrelenting. Ferociously he insisted to the publishers that they *must* reduce his salary to the letter of the contract. For a while he bided his time about finding another publisher, and worked off his indignation by striding round the cliffs near Broadstairs in scorching sunshine for four or five hours at a stretch. His was the pride of a self-made man. Had he not lately, in the very first chapter of *Martin Chuzzlewit*, ridiculed all family trees?

A consolation to him, in his own family circle, was Georgina Hogarth, Kate's fifteen-year-old sister. During the American journey she had helped to care for the children in London, winning their affection, and had now been invited to live with the family, just as her sister Mary had at the same age. She strongly resembled her dead sister, Dickens found, so that 'when she and Kate and I are

Right: Miss Georgina Hogarth painted by Augustus Egg, circa 1850

sitting together, I seem to think that what has happened is a melancholy dream from which I am just awakening. The perfect likeness of what she was, will never be again, but so much of her spirit shines out [in Georgina] that the old time comes back again at some seasons, and I can hardly separate it from the present.' Georgina became a social companion to Dickens, as Mary had been, during Kate's confinements.

Between his monthly instalments of *Martin Chuzzlewit* and the summer in Yorkshire and Broadstairs, Dickens occupied himself with public duties – and one private one, when his parents at last prevailed upon him to fetch them back from Exeter and settle them at Blackheath. The public duties included taking the chair at a meeting called to discuss the establishment of a Society of Authors, advising Angela Burdett Coutts on assistance to a Ragged School in Holborn, and address-ing the Athenaeum Institute in Manchester. It was at the last that the 'bright eyes and beaming faces' of the children gave him the seed of a short book that, in contrast to the acid realism of *Martin Chuzzlewit*, would cheer people's hearts with generous fellowship. He started to write *A Christmas Carol* in October 1843, concurrently with *Martin Chuzzlewit*, and had it finished in time for publication by Christmas that year. Not that the spirit of fellowship wiped away his indigna-tion with Chapman and Hall: they were to publish it as a commission from him, and he paid all the expenses of production.

A Christmas Carol quite consumed his mind during the weeks of its writing. He 'wept and laughed, and wept again, and excited himself in a most extraordinary manner in the composition; and thinking whereof he walked about the black streets of London fifteen and twenty miles many a night when all sober folks had gone to bed'.

And when he had finished it, what Christmas parties there were at Devonshire Terrace! 'Such dinings', he wrote to Felton in Boston, 'such dancings, such con-jurings, such blind-man's-buffings, such theatre-goings, such kissings out of old years and kissings-in of new ones never took place in these parts before.' And to Macready, still in the United States, he wrote 'that Forster and I conjured bravely, that a plum-pudding was produced from an empty saucepan, held over a blazing fire kindled in Stanfield's hat without damage to the lining; that a box of bran was changed into a live guinea-pig, which ran between my godchild's feet, and was the cause of such a shrill uproar and clapping of hands...'

Jane Carlyle, the historian's tart-spirited wife, was at the party, and was bowled over by it. Dickens, she said, was the best conjuror she had ever seen (a hobby that he shared with another, very different Victorian, Isambard Kingdom Brunel), and with Forster he conjured until they were sweating and seemed '*drunk with their efforts*'. The 'gigantic Thackeray' and everyone else capered madly in dances, but Jane Carlyle declined Dickens's invitation to dance with him. After supper, however,

Stave I.

Marley's Ghost.

Marley was dead: to begin with. There is no doubt whatever, about that. The register of his burial was signed by the clergyman, the clerk, the undertaker, and ~~the chief mourner~~ the chief mourner. Scrooge signed it; and Scrooge's name was good upon 'change, for anything he put his hand to. Old Marley was as dead as a door-nail.

Mind! I don't mean to say, that I know, of my own knowledge, what there is particularly dead about a door-nail. I might have been inclined, myself, to regard a coffin-nail as the deadest piece of ironmongery in the trade. But the wisdom of our ancestors is in the simile; and my unhallowed hands shall not disturb it, or the country's done for. You will therefore permit me to repeat, emphatically, that Marley was as dead as a door-nail.

Scrooge knew he was dead. Of course he did. How could it be otherwise? Scrooge and he were partners for I don't know how many years. Scrooge was his sole executor, his sole administrator, his sole assign, his sole residuary legatee: his sole friend and sole mourner. And even Scrooge was not so dreadfully cut up by the sad event, but that he was an excellent man of business on the very day of the funeral, and solemnized it with an undoubted bargain.

The mention of Marley's funeral brings me back to the point I started from. There is no doubt that Marley was dead. This must be distinctly understood, or nothing wonderful can come out of the story I am going to relate. If we were not perfectly convinced that Hamlet's Father died before the play began, there would be nothing more remarkable in his taking a stroll at night, in an easterly wind, upon his own ramparts, than there would be in any other middle-aged gentleman rashly turning out after dark in a breezy spot — say Saint Paul's churchyard for instance — literally to astonish his son's weak mind.

Scrooge never painted out so old Marley's name. There it

when we were all madder than ever with the pulling of crackers, the drinking of champagne, and the making of speeches, a universal country dance was proposed – and Forster
seizing me round the waist, whirled me into the thick of it, and *made* me dance!! like
a person in the tread-mill who must move forward or be crushed to death! Once I cried
out, 'Oh for the love of Heaven let me go! you are going to dash my brains out against
the folding doors!' 'Your *brains*!!' he answered, 'who cares about their brains *here?*
Let them go!'

By midnight the party was 'something not unlike the *rape of the Sabines*!' She
doubted 'there was as much witty speech uttered in all the aristocratic, conventional drawing rooms thro'out London that night as among us little knot of
blackguardist literary people who felt ourselves above all rules, and independent
of the universe!.. the pleasantest company ... *are* the *blackguards*!'

Stoking up all this mad cheerfulness was the news that *A Christmas Carol* had
sold six thousand copies at five shillings its first day in the bookshops and promised
to sell many more. Not only the popular readership took to the little book, buying
it and writing Dickens letters of gratitude; Thackeray was declaring him to be
'the master of all the English humourists now alive', and the book a 'national
benefit, and to every man or woman who reads it a personal kindness'. Lord Jeffrey, pouring 'blessings on your kind heart', wrote to Dickens that he had done
more good with the book than the whole of the Christian Church could in a year.
'I want', Jeffrey added, 'amazingly to see you rich and independent of all irksome
exertions.'

That is just what Dickens wanted for himself, and now could anticipate. He
started to plan another trip abroad, this time to somewhere free of the afflictions
that had beset him in America: to Italy, he decided, having lately begun to teach
himself a little of the language. There in the idle sunlight of the Mediterranean,
with no deadline shadowing him, he could write '*such* a story, all at once, no parts,
sledge-hammer blow'.

For the time being, the blows turned out to be contrary ones, upon himself.
In February he opened the *Christmas Carol* statement from Chapman and Hall,
and instead of the £1000 he expected there was £230, with perhaps as much again
to come from later sales. The publishers, once the 'best of booksellers', were now
'preposterously ignorant of all the essentials of their business'. They had scarcely
bothered to advertise the book at all. That he had himself insisted upon a beautifully produced edition with four colour plates was no extenuation: 'I have not
the least doubt that they have run the expenses up anyhow purposely to bring
me back.' Naturally his determination to have done with Chapman and Hall was
redoubled, and he opened negotiations with the printers Bradbury and Evans.

Some damage had been done to the sales of *A Christmas Carol* by a pirated
edition. Dickens had put up with previous piracies, as the law on copyright was
patchy; in the case of theatrical plagiarism, particularly, there was nothing he

*Opposite: A page from the
manuscript of* A Christmas
Carol

Right: 'Mr Fezziwig's Ball'. An illustration by John Leech for A Christmas Carol

Right: 'Mr Fezziwig's Ball'. An illustration by John Leech for A Christmas Carol

Opposite top: 'The Pickwickian's Start from the Bull at Rochester' by Cecil Aldin
Opposite bottom: Cruikshank's original water-colour for 'Oliver introduced to the respectable Old Gentleman'.

could do to stop it, and instead he sometimes did his best to make such productions decently faithful to his work by helping the producer. The printed piracy of *A Christmas Carol* uncapped all the resentment he had felt on this score: it was, as Vice-Chancellor Knight Bruce agreed, hearing the argument for an injunction, a case of 'peculiar flagrancy'. The pirates claimed to have 're-originated' and improved the story: in fact, such few changes as they had made were described by Dickens, in the application drafted by his counsel, Thomas Talfourd, thus: 'You use my ideas as gipsies do stolen children; disfigure them and then make them pass for their own.' The injunction was granted, but Dickens was foiled in his suit for damages (which he pursued in disregard of threats from dark strangers sent to menace him) by the publishers' flight into bankruptcy. The busi-

Original Sketch

George Cruikshank

ness cost him £700, more than the profit he could see from the book itself. 'It is better to suffer a great wrong', he concluded, 'than to have recourse to the much greater wrong of the law.'

He was now seriously short of money. His unpaid bills were 'terrific', and on 15 January 1844, a fifth baby, Francis, had been born. Still Dickens would not climb down from his rage with Chapman and Hall. The publishers learned that the book edition of *Martin Chuzzlewit* would be their last dealings with him. He reached an agreement with Bradbury and Evans whereby they advanced him £2800 in return for a twenty-five per cent interest in all his work for eight years to come. Nor would he go without the Italian holiday. He would find means of reducing his expenses – a family of seven, the servants, rent and rates at Devonshire Terrace, endless dinners and parties, equally endless demands from his parents, and occasionally from his brothers – let the house, and then, off to 'such Italian castles, bright in sunny days, and pale in moonlight nights, as I am building in the air!'.

A restlessness in Dickens had now become very marked and was never to

Above: The meeting at the Liverpool Mechanics' Institute presided over by Dickens with Christiana Weller at the piano

Opposite top: An illustration by George Cattermole for The Old Curiosity Shop
Opposite bottom: 'The Grave of Little Nell' by George Cattermole

127

dwindle. Such part of it as may not be traced to his childhood was attributable to the dissatisfaction he felt with Kate. There is no evidence that he was yet able to face that dissatisfaction squarely. As for several years now, he expressed it in occasional asperities – a 'donkey' he called her in a letter to Mrs Colden – and in a susceptibility to flirting. At Liverpool in February 1844 to address the Mechanics' Institute, he had to introduce a 'young lady whom I have some difficulty and tenderness in announcing – Miss Weller'. Looking round from the laughing audience, Dickens saw that he had managed to embarrass a delicately beautiful girl, in whose face, watching his, he 'saw an angel's message ... that smote me to the heart'. After she had played, most strikingly, he invited her to bring her father and have lunch with him the next day, which she did. Before he left Liverpool, Dickens wrote a few verses to her. To his friend in Liverpool, T. J. Thompson, he reproached himself as a 'madman' for the 'incredible feeling I have conceived for that girl'.

A week later, in London, he received a letter in which Thompson declared that he himself had fallen in love with Christiana Weller and asked for Dickens's advice about approaching her father. Dickens felt 'my very lips turn white', but advised Thompson not to hesitate. A month later they were engaged and, after several broken and re-made engagements, were married the following year. Dickens attended their wedding, but soon afterwards was complaining that Christiana had 'a devil of a whimpering, pouting temper ... a mere spoiled child'. Later Dickens's brother Fred married Christiana's sister Anna, despite Dickens's by now grave doubts concerning the Weller family's generic character.

Chapter Fourteen

Out of My Proper Soil

EARLY IN JULY A 'VAST PHANTOM' ROLLED DOWN THE DOVER road, a shabby old coach 'about the size of your library', as Dickens described it to Forster, 'with night-lamps and day-lamps and pockets and imperials and leathern cellars, and the most extraordinary contrivances'. It had cost £45 and required four horses. Inside were Dickens, Kate, the five children, Georgina, the maid Anne, a cook, two nurses for the children, and a French courier named Roche.

They crossed to Boulogne, rolled on through Paris, Burgundy, to Lyons, then took a steamer down the Rhône to Avignon, rolled again through Aix-en-Provence to Marseilles, where the carriage was hoisted on board a steamship to Genoa. At every hotel they were greeted with rapture that reached a crescendo of applause when the baby was produced, and bidden farewell after a no less enthusiastic argument between Roche and the landlord over the bill. Dickens's pleasure in the journey was reinforced by his gladness to be out of England. He had left his country with something like a curse:

I declare, [he wrote to Forster] I never go into what is called 'society' that I am not aweary of it, despise it, hate it, and reject it. The more I see of its extraordinary conceit, and its stupendous ignorance of what is passing out of doors, the more certain I am that it is approaching the period when, being incapable of reforming itself, it will have to submit to be reformed by others off the face of the earth.

Dickens was never the man to criticize his own country by adulating others. The French cities he thought 'unscavengered'. The Catholic Church was dying in its long sleep. As for the relics of the Inquisition at Avignon, 'Gurgle, swill, bloat, burst, for the Redeemer's honour! Suck the bloody rag, deep down into your unbelieving body, Heretic, at every breath you draw!'

At first sight, Genoa was a disappointment, the city dirty and decaying, the house reserved for them outside Genoa, the Villa di Bella Vista, a 'pink jail.... A mighty old, wandering, ghostly, echoing, grim, bare house', the stable so alive with 'vermin and swarmers, that I always expect to see the carriage going out bodily, with legion of industrious fleas harnessed to and drawing it off, on their own account'. But next morning the sun was shining from a blue sky on a deeper blue sea, and with Roche Dickens set about arranging the house to suit them until somewhere better could be found. Once he had accustomed himself to the heat, he was off exploring the life of the countryside and of the swarming city, the sea-shore and the grand, mouldering villas. He was soon fluent enough in Italian with the help of some lessons to be 'as bold as a lion in the streets. The audacity with which one begins to speak when there is no help for it, is quite astonishing.'

His visit to Italy would be private, in contrast to the American journey, but he had some introductions in Genoa, through which he met, among others, the Marquis di Negri, who had been a friend of Byron. From a reception one night at the Marquis's grottoed villa Dickens had to run home if he was to get out of Genoa before the city gates were locked. In the darkness he fell over a pole 'headlong, with such force that I rolled myself completely white in the dust; but although I tore my clothes to shreds, I hardly scratched myself except in one place on the knee'. The fall, however, brought on a recurrence of the old kidney spasms, and he took things easily for a while until he was fit to resume swimming in the 'little blue bay just below the house here, like a fish in high spirits'. Meanwhile his pens, ink, paper, and desk ornaments had been retrieved from the customs house, and he started to consider a Christmas book.

In early September, Dickens went to Marseilles to meet his brother Fred, who was joining them for a fortnight. On his first day at the villa Fred swam too far out, into the current, and was rescued by a fishing boat that happened to be passing. 'It was a world of horror and anguish crowded into four or five minutes', Dickens wrote to Forster, while Georgina, the children and their nurse 'were on a rock in full view of it all, crying, as you may suppose, like mad creatures'.

By the end of the month, they were all installed in a complete floor of a much finer house, the Palazzo Peschiere, with frescoes by Michelangelo. Dickens sat by a window that looked out over goldfish pools and lemon and orange trees, across the steepled bowl of Genoa harbour to the distant Alps, and wondered why he could not make a start on his Christmas story. 'Never did I so stagger upon a threshold before', he told Forster. 'I seem as if I had plucked myself out of my proper soil.... Put me down on Waterloo Bridge at eight o'clock in the evening, with leave to roam about as long as I like, and I would come home, as you know, panting to go on.'

In his anxiety and the strangeness of the place, he dreamed of Mary again. After a night made restless by the pain in his back, he fell asleep very late, and was visited by a spirit draped in blue like a Madonna. Knowing it to be Mary, he wept, and stretched his arms out, calling the apparition 'Dear'. The spirit retreated from the word, but compassionately. He asked for a token of this visitation, the answer to a question, What is the true religion? Was any religion true, or was, perhaps, Roman Catholicism the best? The spirit answered tenderly, 'For *you*, it is the best.' He woke up with his cheeks washed by tears.

At last it was the interminably clanging bells of Genoa, driving him giddy with his inability to concentrate, which gave him the clue to his story – gave him the title, his invariable starting-point: *The Chimes*. It would, he told Forster, be 'a great blow for the poor'. Now it rushed out of him 'in a regular, ferocious excite-

Right: '*The Spirits of the Bells*'. *The title page by Maclise for* The Chimes

The Spirits of the Bells.

ment'. He was up at seven, took a cold bath and breakfast, and worked till three –
longer if it rained, which it often did in a stormy October. Typically, 'in pure
determination to get the better of it, I walked twelve miles in mountain rain.'
When the Governor of the province asked, 'Where's the great poet? I want to
see the great poet', and was told he was working and begged to be excused, the
Governor, according to Dickens, answered, ' "Excuses! I wouldn't interfere with
such an occupation for all the world. Pray tell him that my house is open to the
honour of his presence when it is perfectly convenient to him; but not otherwise.
And let no gentleman," said the Governor, a-surweyin' of his suite with a majestic
eye, "call upon Signor Dickens till he is understood to be disengaged." '

With no distractions, Dickens so threw himself into the story that 'my cheeks,
which were beginning to fill out, have sunk again; my hair is very lank; my eyes
have grown immensely large; and the head inside the hair is hot and giddy ...
I have undergone as much sorrow and agitation as if the thing were real; and

*Left: Trotty Veck by John
Leech*

have wakened up with it at night.' It was written in a month. Finishing, 'in a spirit bearing some affinity to those of truth and mercy, and to shame the cruel and canting', Dickens wept, so that his face swelled up 'to twice its proper size, and was hugely ridiculous'.

Now he chafed with wanting the opinion of his friends in London. There was a pleasant enough time to be had in Genoa with friends they had made and their own box at the opera, but Dickens pined for London, the people and sights of home, just for a few days. And so it was arranged. With Roche, the 'brave Courier' who attended to every need and comfort, he first spent a rainy fortnight touring Parma, Bologna, Verona, and 'the gorgeous and wonderful reality of Venice, beyond the fancy of the wildest dreamer. Opium couldn't build such a place': though Dickens, always seeing the skull beneath the finest skin, also inspected the 'wicked, awful' dungeons and deep torture chambers, and shuddered at what others called 'the good old times'. On they went to Milan, where they had arranged to meet Kate and Georgina. Dickens assured himself about Charley's lessons in French and writing, about the dancing classes that Charley and his sisters were having, and gave Kate and Georgina instructions that at all costs they must be patient with Mrs Macready's young sister, an irritating guest at the Palazzo Peschiere. Now Dickens and Roche headed north, into the Alps, crossing the Simplon Pass in moonlight, the wind blowing the snow into their faces. In a rose-coloured dawn they descended to Switzerland, through Geneva, Basle, Strasbourg and on through mud to Paris, Boulogne, the boat. Nine days after leaving Milan, Dickens, his face red with the winter journey, was embracing Maclise and Forster.

In three days he discussed the manuscript with Forster, made revisions, took it into Bradbury and Evans for printing (though technically it would be published by Chapman and Hall, who had the facilities for distributing the copies), discussed the illustrations, dined at Gore House, lunched with Ainsworth; and then, at Forster's apartments in Lincoln's Inn Fields, a circle of friends were waiting for him to read *The Chimes* to them.

It was a triumph. The journey it had demanded was nothing in comparison to this reward. The word spread, and Dickens had to do other readings. Everybody who heard the story was deeply moved. Dickens wrote to Kate, 'If you had seen Macready last night, undisguisedly sobbing, and crying on the sofa as I read, you would have felt, as I did, what a thing it is to have power.'

The Chimes was a blast against 'the system', the hard hearts and abstract minds of those who followed the laws of primitive capitalism laid down by the political economists of the early nineteenth century. The poor were to labour all the joyless days of their lives and be grateful for subsistence wages, or the system would break down. Those who lived well off the system were not villains, in Dickens's view, but dupes. Unless they tempered their iron laws with justice and human care, the skies would be red with riot.

Just four weeks before Dickens had started to write *The Chimes*, Marx and Engels had met each other for the first time, in Paris, and discussed the same subject for ten days. Marx had read an essay that Engels wrote from Manchester.

It was [says Edmund Wilson in *To The Finland Station*] an original and brilliant discussion of the 'political economy' of the British, which Engels on his side had been reading up. Engels held that the theories of Adam Smith and Ricardo, of MacCulloch and James Mill, were fundamentally hypocritical rationalizations of the greedy motives behind the system of private property which was destroying the British peoples: the Wealth of Nations made most people poor; Free Trade and Competition left the people still enslaved, and consolidated the monopoly of the bourgeoisie on everything that was worth having – all the philosophies of trade themselves only sanctified the huckster's fraud; the discussions of abstract value were kept abstract on purpose to avoid taking cognisance of the actual conditions under which all commercial transactions took place: the exploitation and destruction of the working class, the alternation of prosperity with crisis. Marx at once began to correspond with Engels....

Nothing there to make Macready sob on a sofa, it is true. Dickens's prescriptions

Below: Dickens reading
The Chimes to his friends.
D. Maclise, 1844

were, as Una Pope-Hennessy remarks in her biography, 'extremely vague and hopelessly sentimental' in the eyes of Marx: he launched no attack on the concept of private property, still less any crusade for the dictatorship of the proletariat. Yet 'the mere fact that "Boz" never attempted to conceal or palliate the unpleasant truth that conditions in England were bad, quite as bad as Lord Ashley's reports testified and as Friedrich Engels reported, lifted the novelist, in Marx's esteem, into the category of social reformers.' That he still has that reputation today is testimony not to the precise social observation in his stories, nor to the 'moral awareness' that English critics require, but to what Robert Giddings has called his 'magic alchemy of dream-symbol and depth-psychology', and George Eliot called his 'transcendental unreality and artistic truthfulness' – in a word, his poetry.

Chapter Fifteen

The Wonder of Naples

DICKENS FOUND TIME DURING HIS FEW DAYS IN LONDON TO arrange assistance for the bereaved family of John Overs, a carpenter whose occasional work as a writer Dickens had befriended. Except in America, where he was swamped with peremptory letters demanding that he arrange publication of an enclosed gem, he was generous to aspiring authors with time he could not easily spare.

On his way back to Italy he stopped in Paris. Macready had just arrived to play a season there, and Dickens was introduced to the glittering literati: Victor Hugo, Alexandre Dumas, Gautier, de Vigny, Michelet, Delacroix, and others. After three days he went on to Marseilles, made a stormy crossing to Genoa, and was back with his family in time for Christmas.

Four weeks later he was off again on a three-month journey southwards, this time with Kate. At Pisa he climbed the tower, at Leghorn honoured the grave of Smollett, compared Siena to 'Venice, without the water'. Dickens was pre-occupied most of the time. There was a tension between himself and Kate over Madame de la Rue, the pretty English wife of a Swiss banker in Genoa.

For several years Dickens had been interested in mesmerism, having seen demonstrations on the stage in London, and was acquainted with its exponent, Dr Elliotson. In America he had tried out his own powers on Kate and succeeded in mesmerizing her within two minutes, banishing her headache. Now in Genoa, becoming friendly with the de la Rues, he wished to help Mme de la Rue to overcome a severe nervous tic. Once the experiment had begun, she revealed that she was subject to hallucinations, which Dickens felt she should relate to him under hypnosis. Since the attacks occurred at all hours and frequently in the middle of the night, Dickens was liable to be called from his bed to attend her and not return for several hours. Kate was jealous; Dickens resented her jealousy, being convinced that he was procuring a recovery in his patient. During their journey south, his mind was often in telepathic search of Mme de la Rue's.

One wet and gusty morning at Radicofani, a gothic village on the road to Rome, their carriage was stopped by a tattered flight of men and boys begging. The white-bearded leader gravely warned Dickens against travelling further in the weather that day: the wind would blow them off the mountain. 'Speak to my servant', Dickens replied. 'It's his business, not mine.' '*Santa Maria!*' the old man exclaimed walking off, 'these English Lords, it's not their business if they're killed, they leave it to their servants!' His warning was justified; Dickens and Roche

Left: William Charles Macready, the actor and old friend of Dickens who had kept an eye on the Dickens children during their parents American tour of 1842

had to hang on to the outside of the carriage to prevent the wind from taking it over the edge.

Carnival week in Rome was a riot that Dickens enjoyed, and he was moved by the 'awful beauty, and utter desolation' of the Colosseum. The monuments of medieval Catholicism he thought vulgar. In Naples, what moved him most was the degrading poverty he saw. Here Georgina was joining them: Dickens watched through a telescope her boat come into port, but it was not so much Georgina nor news of the children that he was feverish to see, but the mailbags being unloaded, with a letter in them from M. de la Rue about his wife's condition in Dickens's absence. She was not well, Dickens learned. Still they would all meet again in Rome for Holy Week.

After touring through Sorrento and Pompeii, Dickens led his two imperturbable Victorian womenfolk up Vesuvius on a winter night. Twenty-two guides accompanied them through iced snow and volcanic fire, Dickens walking with a stick, Kate and Georgina carried in a sedan chair. Amid cinder and sulphur and showers of red-hot stones, they approached the roaring, flaming crater. Kate and Georgina waited while Dickens trod the thin crust to the brink, 'looked down into the flaming bowels of the mountain and came back again, alight in half a dozen places, and burnt from head to foot'.

The descent was perilous and along icy precipices, the party walking and skidding with linked hands. Then someone's boots slid from under him, and he carried two others with him over the edge and five hundred feet down, shrieking into the night and silence. 'My ladies' clothes were so torn off their backs that they would not have been decent, if there could have been any thought of such things at such time.... My ladies are the wonder of Naples, and everybody is open-mouthed.'

In Rome again, there were further night-time treatments of Mme de la Rue, causing agitation, of different sorts, in Dickens and in Kate. They all travelled together to Florence after Easter, and back to Genoa. By this time Kate was not

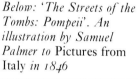

Below: 'The Streets of the Tombs: Pompeii'. An illustration by Samuel Palmer to Pictures from Italy *in 1846*

on speaking terms with Mme de la Rue. The experimental obsession that had gripped Dickens in his daily mesmerisms, and M. de la Rue's gratitude, did nothing to convince Kate that her jealousy was groundless. She shouted at Dickens and wept, while he flatly refused to abandon his experiments just to placate her. In the end, Kate's state of mind was so patent that Dickens could no longer conceal it from the de la Rues. They were tactful. He was humiliated.

Yet without forgetting the humiliation, he made plans to give Kate a delightful surprise when they were back at Devonshire Terrace. She would find the house redecorated. Dickens's anxieties about money had been blown away by the news from London. *The Chimes* was a brilliant success, with an immediate profit of nearly £1500; and a further sum of nearly £1000 was due to him from Chapman and Hall from continued sales of the earlier books.

By early June the 'vast phantom' was being packed again at the Palazzo Peschiere. Dickens was not there: he was staying with the de la Rues, teaching M. de la Rue how to mesmerize his wife.

On its way home the carriage was lighter than it had been by one passenger: the cook had fallen in love with a French cook and was to marry him. They intended to open a restaurant in Genoa. Dickens thought it a dubious business, and, characteristically thoughtful, made provision for the cook to return to England if things did not work out. 'The man hasn't a penny. If there were an opening for a nice clean restaurant in Genoa – which I don't believe there is, for the Genoese have a natural enjoyment of dirt, garlic, and oil – it would still be a very hazardous venture, as the priests will certainly damage the man, if they can, for marrying a Protestant woman.'

Everything he had seen of the Catholic Church fed his opinion of its malevolence, a political arm against the poor and ignorant. Its rituals struck him as a tawdry pantomime in comparison to a Church of England service. Edgar Johnson comments, 'He did not analyze *as* traditional what was traditional in his own feelings; where he recognized tradition at all he disliked it as obstructive and reactionary; and he made no endeavour to understand its emotional power when he found it embodied in strange and alien forms.'

The Italian people, however, had charmed him. Arriving in Switzerland, he remarked on the cleanliness, 'wonderful to those who come from Italy. But the beautiful Italian manners, the sweet language, the quick recognition of a pleasant look or cheerful word; the captivating expression of a desire to oblige in everything; these are left behind the Alps. Remembering them, I sigh for the dirt again: the brick floors, bare walls, unplastered ceilings, and broken windows.'

The passage into Switzerland down from the Great St Gotthard Pass had been the most dangerous thing that a carriage and horses can do. We had two great wooden logs for drags, and snapped them both like matches. The road is like a geometrical staircase, with horrible depths beneath it; and at every turn it is a toss-up, or seems to be, whether the leaders shall go round or over. The lives of the whole party may depend upon a strap in the harness; and if we broke our rotten harness once yesterday, we broke it at least a dozen times.

The horses slithered about, dragging the carriage against the rocks and tangling the harness 'like a skein of thread. We broke two thick iron chains, and crushed the box of a wheel, as it was; and the carriage is now undergoing repair.'

In spite of all such hazards and struggles, Dickens had thoroughly enjoyed the year in Italy. He was a private tourist, not a social observer or paraded celebrity, as he had been in America. And the Italians, though polite and respectful to him, never forgot him. When he died, the headline in the Genoese newspaper was '*Il nostro Carlo Dickens è morto*'.

Chapter Sixteen

Fighting the Battle

THE YEAR OF LEISURE IN ITALY HAD NOT YIELDED THAT 'sledge-hammer blow' of a novel that Dickens had anticipated, nor did he give himself the chance of writing it now that he was back in his haunts. Probably he required the spur of a deadline. As though deliberately avoiding the task, he now spent the second half of 1845 in pursuits that drained all the energy he had.

The first enthusiasm was a play to be acted privately by his friends with Dickens, of course, as stage manager, director, and star. He had mentioned the idea to Forster on his visit to London from Italy, and now settled on Ben Jonson's *Every Man in his Humour*. The part of the braggart Bobadil, one of Jonson's greatest creations, he himself would play; the jealous Kitely was Forster; others in the cast were T. J. Thompson, Mark Lemon, Douglas Jerrold (author of *Black-ey'd Susan*), the artists Cruikshank, John Leech, Cattermole, Frank Stone, and Dickens's brothers Fred and Augustus. Two other artists, Maclise and Stanfield, were overcome by stage fright early in rehearsals (though Maclise was persuaded to appear in a repeat performance, and half-fainted with nerves). Stanfield became the designer. Throughout the rehearsals Dickens was 'half dead with Managerial work', attending to everything, from whipping on the 'utterly careless and unbusiness-like set of dogs' (Forster not excepted) who were his cast, to numbering the seats and hammering up the set. 'It is ludicrous the fuss the actors make about this play', Macready thought; they 'seemed to be under a perfect delusion as to their degree of skill and power in an art of which they do not know what may be called the very rudiments.'

On 20 September the invited audience of some two hundred in the private theatre in Soho included Lady Holland, the Duke of Devonshire, and Tennyson, who had made the journey from Lincolnshire. Thomas and Jane Carlyle did not think much of the evening: Forster merely imitated Macready (an accusation often made about Forster off stage too), and Dickens was affected. Macready delivered himself of faint praise, conceding that 'several of the actors were very fine as amateurs'. But the buzz went around town that it had really been an extraordinary affair, especially Dickens in his armour, spurred boots, and mustachios and the company were prevailed upon to repeat the play. This time they took the much larger St James Theatre, intending to give the swollen receipts to a charity. The audience was even more distinguished, including Prince Albert, Prince George, Wellington, the insatiable Duke of Devonshire, and the Hon. Mrs Caroline Norton accompanied by Lord Melbourne, who was heard in an interval to remark,

'I knew this play would be dull, but that it should be so damnably dull as this I did not suppose.' The noble lord did not know how lightly he was let off: Thackeray had offered to sing between the acts and was wounded when his offer was declined. A few weeks later, at New Year, the undaunted company gave another benefit performance, this time of *The Elder Brother* by Massinger and Fletcher.

At the same time as he was producing Jonson's play, Dickens was thinking about starting a new weekly periodical to be called *The Cricket*. Apart from his lifelong devotion to the periodical miscellany form (probably deriving from a set of Goldsmith's *The Bee*, a parting present given to him by William Giles, the Chatham schoolmaster), Dickens was concerned about stabilizing his income again, with Kate pregnant for the sixth time. Forster deterred him from this project, but it seeded the idea of Dickens's Christmas story that year, *The Cricket on the Hearth*, which he began to write in October.

Instead of starting a new periodical, Dickens's attention now turned to an enormous new project. He had, in the past, more than once thought of returning to his first profession, journalism, but in the editor's chair this time. He saw no daily

Below left: A poster advertising Every Man in his Humour *with sketches by Maclise of Dickens as Bobadil and Forster as Kitely*
Below right: As Captain Bobadil in Every Man in his Humour

newspaper in the country that was 'fighting the battle staunchly' for the Liberal Party and also serving the true needs of the common people, no paper he would wish to edit. Why not create one? Before going to Italy, partly piqued by the *Morning Chronicle*'s refusal to pay him ten guineas a time for letters from abroad, he had had preliminary talks with Forster, Bradbury and Evans, and Joseph Paxton, a railway magnate who had started his working life as the Duke of Devonshire's gardener. Now he reopened the talks, and at the same time busied himself with interrogating all his newspaper connections about the precise details of administration that would be entailed.

His nose for the ripe time was as keen as ever. The famine in Ireland and a rainy harvest in England were splitting the Tory government apart on the question of the Corn Laws. Richard Cobden's cogent speeches in the Commons drove in the wedge, and the Prime Minister himself, Sir Robert Peel, was converted. Other pressures for change were at work: a slump in business, poverty in the cities and the countryside, the dreadful conditions in mine and factory. Something of this Dickens had seen for himself. How he would enjoy bending the ears of government to what he would have to say every morning.

Below: As editor of the new, liberal newspaper the Daily News *in 1846*

By the end of October, when Alfred d'Orsay Tennyson Dickens was born and named for his godfathers, the capital to launch the new paper was in sight. Bradbury and Evans, Paxton and some leading Liberals in the north would get further backing from a finance house that could command plenty of commercial support through advertisements. Dickens had begun to recruit a staff. Managing the news room would be his father, now as orotund in body as in speech, but always an efficient manager of anything save his own money. Kate's father was the music and theatre critic. The gossip columnist was Lady Blessington. The majority of the staff were distinguished journalists with long experience on other newspapers, from whom they were seduced by rates of pay well above the normal. 'A powerful combination of energy, experience, and money', Dickens thought it all, and chuckled at the alarm among the rest of the daily press, particularly *The Times*.

At the top of the organization, editing the paper, he had always imagined himself, but for a time, during the setting-up, reserved his decision. Forster was against it, arguing that Dickens stood to gain little in fame from the position, and to lose his freedom in political commitments. Finally, however, Dickens informed Bradbury and Evans that he would edit the paper at twice the £1000 salary that had been estimated. His politics would be corporative, seeking to unite the country in reform, not pitting class against class, or playing party-political games.

Then for a week or two Dickens was convinced the enterprise was 'a doomed thing', following the collapse of a broking house which brought down with it some backers and advertisers. 'It would end in your Ruin', he warned Bradbury and Evans. They disagreed (correctly, as history shows), and persuaded him to resume the project, with their trust in Dickens's cool judgement perhaps a little shaken.

At Christmas *The Times* savaged *The Cricket on the Hearth*. There, Forster told Macready, it just proved what he had said to Dickens, no good could come of his editing the new paper: but, he went on, Dickens was so 'intensely fixed on his own opinions, and in his admiration of his own works' that he paid no attention to Forster's advice or anyone's criticisms, and 'this partial passion would grow upon him, till it became an incurable evil'. Dickens's own opinions – '*The Times* has done it a great deal of service' – looked better when the book swiftly reached double the sales of its Christmas predecessors.

Peel had resigned his office in November; the Whigs were unwilling to fight the repeal of the Corn Laws through the Lords, so Peel was reappointed and formed a new Cabinet. On 20 January he would address the House. That night, amid the turmoil of a refurbished printing house and briefly rehearsed printers, the first issue of the *Daily News* came off the press, attended by agitated proprietors. Peel had embraced Cobden's views. Ten thousand people in Fleet Street wanted to pay 5d for what Dickens's paper would say, and many thousands elsewhere in the country.

It was a messy production, but there was eloquence. The leader-writer W. J. Fox, 'golden-tongued apostle of untaxed bread', denounced the Corn Laws. A poem declaimed 'The Wants of the People'. Dickens contributed a Travelling Letter, the first of several created from the letters he had written from Italy. The first day's circulation was of course largely due to novelty-appeal, but the sale steadied out at four thousand which compared well with all other papers except *The Times*'s twenty-five thousand.

By the time the *Daily News* was properly established, however, Dickens no longer sat in its offices. Circumstances chafed him – faulty printing, editorial disagreements, the potentially corrupt influence of the railway interests embodied in Paxton, and most of all the suspicious Bradbury's persistence in meddling with Dickens's arrangements and contradicting his appointments – but quite likely Dickens had suddenly lost his taste for the responsibility when it was served up so lavishly, and not under the absolute control he was used to but scrutinized by the proprietors of capital. 'I have been revolving plans in my mind this morning', he wrote to Forster only a week after the first issue, 'for quitting the paper and going abroad again to write a new book in shilling numbers.'

Right: A cartoon from Mephystopheles *parodying Landseer's 'A Midsummer's Night's Dream' and poking fun at the rivalry between the* Daily News *and the established 'dailies'*

TITANIA DICKENS TO BOTTOM, THE DAILY NEWS.

Come rest in this bosom, my own stricken donkey,
Nor heed *Times*, nor *Chronicle*, *Graudn'a*, nor *Flunkey*;
Though the leaders are scorned of my own *Daily News*,
I who wrote them, to read them will never refuse.
What's an editor made for, if he isn't the brick,
Circulation or none, to his paper to stick ?

I know not, I ask not, if they buy you or not,
I but know that I edit thee—therefore they ought.
Thou hast called me thy " Dickens " in moments of bliss,
Still *the* Dickens I'll play with thee even in this ;
While there's shot in the locker thy fortune is mine,
While a copper is left I am *thy* Valentine !

After editing the first seventeen issues of the *Daily News*, he invited Forster, an experienced journalist, to take over his chair. Forster was pleased to accept, raising unworthy doubts whether that had not been in his mind before. Dickens assured Bradbury and Evans that his author's relationship with them would not be affected. Nor would he allow his resignation to be seen as an act of hostility against the paper he had founded, and which his closest friend now edited. He contributed six more Travelling Letters, which, with additions, and illustrated by Samuel Palmer, were published as a book, *Pictures from Italy*, by Bradbury and Evans in May. For the paper he also wrote about the Ragged Schools, and about capital punishment, arguing that it deterred no criminals, incited some by its morbid glamour, on occasion murdered the innocent, and worst of all degraded the spectators. So concerned was he about the law and society at this time, that he considered qualifying as a magistrate.

Still revolving in his mind was the new book he had mentioned to Forster, and at last, nearly two years after finishing *Martin Chuzzlewit*, in April 1846 he agreed to write a novel in twenty monthly parts for Bradbury and Evans.

Chapter Seventeen

Want of Something

THE RESTLESSNESS IN DICKENS'S CHARACTER WAS NOW SO
marked that it was clearly a symptom of a deep disturbance. No sooner had he
made his abrupt about-turn at the *Daily News* than he could not abide London
any more. Kate refused to return to Genoa and the de la Rues, and so the choice
was Lausanne, conveniently close across the Alps.

Before they left, at the end of May, there was a hectic series of dinners, some
to say farewell to friends, others charitable occasions at which Dickens presided.
His public statements about charity all tended to promote 'sweet accord and harmony among all classes', through popular education and enlightenment. When
Forster, having supplied ham sandwiches for a company and finding a quantity
left over, instructed his servant to distribute them among poor women but first
to 'institute close enquiry into their life, conduct, and behaviour', Dickens roared
with amusement, but his own charitable provisions, on the far greater scale that
Miss Coutts's money could achieve, were no less paternalistic. Fallen women were
to be taught 'habits of firmness and self-restraint', encouraged by the offer, when
they were redeemed, of being sent to the colonies with a view to marriage. It
was all of a piece with the editorial programme of the *Daily News* and with middle-
class opinion in the country, where, in contrast to the imminent revolution in
France, the Chartists' petition did not disturb the steady tide of renewed prosperity. It was, however, in contradiction to Dickens's own inner sentiments, as
they were now to be expressed in *Dombey and Son*. The solidly middle-class businessman Dombey is unquestionably drawn as a symbol of the 'moral pestilence'
that corroded English society: a man who, as in *The Chimes*, is analysed as no
villain, simply a smug, unaware tool of a cold-hearted economic doctrine by which
all human relationships were determined by cash. Such a society is not to be
redeemed by paternalistic charities.

Deeper still, in Dickens's state of disturbance, was his own relationship with
Kate. Throughout all his novels, scarcely any marriage, or home life, considered
at length is a happy one. The unhappy pursuit of Maria Beadnell had developed
in him a romantic need for innocence in love; the young death of Mary Hogarth
had fixed it. Georgina served as a sentimental reminder of her sister: the flirtations with older women were innocent ones. Kate did not serve any neurotic need.
Her plump and lethargic body was fertile, and every pregnancy, increasingly received by him with low comedy, was a new demand on Dickens's earnings, albeit
he was a wonderful father to children while they were small. And Kate's mind,

*Opposite: Florence Dombey
by W. M. Egley*

150

in contrast, was not fertile enough to give Dickens any intellectual stimulation. She did not understand him, as her jealousy of his treatment of Mme de la Rue testifies. He was condescending to her, bound by fatherhood and convention to stick with her but tormented by what he later called the 'unhappy loss or want of something'. After his death, his daughter Katey said: 'My father did not understand women.'

The house was rented again, and off they went steaming down the Rhine, on through Switzerland to Lausanne, where they found a little bijou house, smothered with roses, on the shore of Lake Geneva. A month after leaving London, Dickens had got the title of the new book, *Dombey and Son*, was issuing orders about illustrations, and at the same time was thinking about the theme of an abandoned battleground for his Christmas book. Meanwhile there were games and excursions with the children, sailing and parties. He made his customary tour of the public institutions, glad to find that the prison had abolished the rule of silence, horrified by the ancient instruments of torture at Chillon, sceptical of the 'humbug' monks at Great St Bernard. The distinction between a Protestant canton and a Catholic one he thought plain for all to see:

On the Protestant side, neatness; cheerfulness; industry; education; continual aspiration, at least, after better things. On the Catholic side, dirt, disease, ignorance, squalor, and misery. I have so constantly observed the like of this, since I first came abroad, that I have a sad misgiving that the religion of Ireland lies as deep at the root of all its sorrows, even as English misgovernment and Tory villainy.

Around him he discovered a busy colony of English residents and visitors: William Haldimand, an author; the Hon. Mr Richard Watson (like Haldimand, a former MP) and his wife; his old friend T.J. Thompson and his once entrancing, now spoiled, wife Christiana. Visitors included Ainsworth, Tennyson, Brunel, and the political economist Nassau Senior. Their interest in what he was writing prompted him to give them a reading of the first instalment, and it went so well that he wrote to Forster, 'a great deal of money might possibly be made (if it were not infra dig) by one's having Readings of one's own books. It would be an *odd* thing.' Odd or not, the idea was later to grip him with mortal persistence.

The writing of *Dombey* was not going as well.

Invention, thank God, seems the easiest thing in the world, and I seem to have such a preposterous sense of the ridiculous, after this long rest, as to be constantly requiring to restrain myself from launching into extravagances in the height of my enjoyment. But the difficulty of going at what I call a rapid pace is prodigious: it is almost an impossibility. I suppose this is partly the effect of two years' ease, and partly of the absence of streets.

Again, as in Genoa, he was missing London, his London. The concurrent work on his Christmas book also jaded him: 'I am sick, giddy, and capriciously

Opposite: Charles Dickens painted in 1859 by W. P. Frith

despondent. I have bad nights; am full of disquietude and anxiety; and am constantly haunted by the idea that I am wasting the marrow of the larger book, and ought to be at rest.' Was it, he wondered, the sluggish lakeside atmosphere that held him up? Twice, stimulating himself with a change of scene, he spent some weeks in Geneva, working. It was there he described Mrs Pipchin's dame-school: 'It is from the life, and I was there – I don't suppose I was eight years old. . . . We should be devilish sharp in what we do to children.'

By the middle of October he had finished his Christmas book, *The Battle Of Life*, the story of two similar sisters who love the same man and are both loved by him. That the sisters' names, Marion and Grace, start with the same initials as Mary and Georgina is a clue, if clue were needed, of what dreams and regrets Dickens was embalming in rich sentiment, closing with the wish to go on 'talking often of old times'. 'A wretched affair', Thackeray called it, and few critics disagreed, except the many thousands of readers who bought it in still greater numbers than its Christmas predecessors.

However, they were also buying the instalments of *Dombey*, Dickens's first novel about 'a complete way of living', according to J.B. Priestley, 'an important experiment in fiction, leading the way for later novelists'. The success of the opening number, Dickens reported to Forster, 'is BRILLIANT', exceeding his extremest hope of thirty thousand. Encouraged, in the middle of November he moved his family to Paris, trusting that 'the life and crowd of that extraordinary place will come vividly to my assistance in writing'. They rented an eccentrically elaborate house in the Faubourg St Honoré, for a winter so cold that the bedroom water-jugs split with ice.

Again he could not get started, 'went about it and about, and dodged at it, like a bird with a lump of sugar'. He walked all over Paris as though it were London, despising the insouciance he noted in that 'wicked and detestable place, though wonderfully attractive'. Then he did get started again, and felt able to take a quick trip to London in the middle of December. *The Battle of Life* was being staged, as all the Christmas books had been (and most of the others), and the production was 'in a state so horrible . . . the densest and most insufferable nonsense', that he had to sit down with the cast and perform the script right through for them.

He was back in Paris for Christmas, completing the death of Paul Dombey. That episode 'amazed Paris'. At home, Lord Jeffrey was deeply moved again, 'and felt my heart purified by those tears'. Thackeray, who found most of Dickens's work too broadly brushed, had just started to write *Vanity Fair*; he rushed into the offices of *Punch*, threw the new instalment of *Dombey* down on Mark Lemon's desk, and declared, 'There's no writing against such power as this. One has no chance.' Dickens himself, 'had no hope of getting to sleep' after writing the episode, so 'went out, and walked about Paris until breakfast time next morn-

Opposite: The frontispiece by Phiz to Dombey and Son *showing Florence and Paul Dombey on the seashore*

Right: A preliminary drawing by John Leech for The Battle of Life, *Dickens's fourth Christmas book*

ing', when he met Forster, who was arriving for a holiday after resigning from the *Daily News* and its quarrelsome proprietors.

Together the two friends spent a fortnight devouring all the sights and spectacles of Paris, and meeting many celebrities: Chateaubriand, Lamartine, Dumas, Gautier and Victor Hugo, who, in his apartment 'like an old curiosity shop', was just embarking on *Les Misérables*. Dickens and Hugo had much respect for each other's work.

When he returned to England, Forster took Dickens's son Charles with him. Miss Coutts had offered to pay for him to go to Eton, and he was to be prepared for the entrance in London. Soon his father joined him in London, on a visit to see the printers, and together they dined at Gore House, where the boy Charles was talked to by Prince Louis Napoleon, later Emperor of France.

No sooner had Dickens returned to Paris than he had to travel to London again with Kate, young Charles having gone down with scarlet fever. They decided not to return to Paris, and rented a house until their own should be vacant again. Kate was pregnant, and on 18 April 1847 was delivered of a son named Sydney Smith Haldimand.

Through all these convulsions, Dickens contrived to complete his instalments of *Dombey*, but at the cost of 'a low dull nervousness'. With Kate he recuperated at Brighton for a fortnight. Then he was back in London for a few weeks, and off to Broadstairs with his family.

In London he helped to smooth out a quarrel between Forster and Thackeray arising from parodies of contemporary novelists that the latter was writing for *Punch*. In consequence, either Thackeray or Bradbury and Evans, the proprietors of *Punch*, thought it wise not to include Dickens among those parodied. Dickens affected to be piqued by the omission, but privately thought that Thackeray did the literary profession no good when he behaved in such a way. Dickens himself took care not to snipe at his fellow writers.

It was in order to benefit writers who were short of money that Dickens now threw himself once more into amateur dramatics. He gathered together his company of friends, and bullied and jollied them through fresh rehearsals of *Every Man in His Humour*, arranged sets, props and costumes, fixed dates for performances in Manchester and Liverpool. They took place at the end of July, and showed a profit, after expenses, of 400 guineas.

Below: William Makepeace Thackeray, photographed in 1863

Dickens's own financial situation was solidly underwritten by the income from *Dombey* and the continuing profits from all his previous books, of most of which he now controlled half the copyright. He would never again be without a substantial sum in the bank. Yet he felt constrained to produce another Christmas book, as much 'not to leave any gap at Christmas firesides' as for the money it would bring him. But it was still not easy for him to write as copiously as he had written a few years earlier; even at Broadstairs he was excruciated by the street musicians who played outside the house all day. Finally, his deep commitment to *Dombey* overcame what he felt to be his Christmas duty, and he relinquished the short book for a year.

Outside his writing hours, the restlessness did not abate. Once the benefit productions in Lancashire were finished, he was 'at a great loss for means of blowing my superfluous steam off . . . but that is always my misfortune'. At the end of the year, after a visit to Edinburgh (where Kate had a miscarriage), he called his

Thespians together once more, this time with a view to raising money for a project of buying Shakespeare's house at Stratford-upon-Avon as a national property. They started to rehearse Beaumont and Fletcher's *Beggar's Bush* but some of the company disagreed with the choice of play and wished to do Goldsmith's *Good-Natured Man*. When that too met with disfavour and two further plays were in turn rejected, Dickens crossly withdrew from the whole business. He retreated to Brighton, and there finished writing *Dombey and Son* in March 1848. That done, he was persuaded to pick up the pieces of the benefit production once more. He could not bear 'the labour of being idle'.

For months he toiled at the plays, which it was now agreed would be the Ben Jonson again and *The Merry Wives of Windsor*, decorated with a few one-act farces. He occupied himself with all the minutest details of management, planning, and publicity, as well as fastidiously directing daily rehearsals and preparing himself to play Justice Shallow in the Shakespeare to Mark Lemon's Falstaff. The two productions at the Haymarket Theatre – Victoria and Albert attended the second – were loudly applauded, and further bookings were accepted for Manchester, Liverpool, Birmingham, Edinburgh and Glasgow. Throughout the journeys, for which the railway company supplied a free pass, Dickens radiated 'brightness and enjoyment', according to Mary Cowden Clarke, who played Mistress Quickly (the other actresses were professional). He told stories, leapt around platforms, shunted his merry group up and down. On stage he was reckoned to be unforgettably comic, ad-libbing with Lemon like a music-hall comedian. (Something of that improvisation may have spilled over into a private evening he spent at Forster's apartment with Carlyle and R.W. Emerson. The two Englishmen shocked the American philosopher with their assurances that in their country few men indeed were chaste before marriage.)

The benefit performances showed a profit of over £2500, and it was given to a bankrupt dramatist, J.S. Knowles. That extraordinary sum did not represent Dickens's motives in undertaking so much work. More eloquent was the relapse of his spirits afterwards. 'I have no energy whatever, I am very miserable. I loathe domestic hearths. I yearn to be a vagabond.'

Events close to him made matters worse. He was saddened by two deaths: 'the brave Courier' Roche, and Lord Jeffrey, an unstinting admirer. But the severest blow since Mary Hogarth's death was the fatal illness, with tuberculosis, of his sister Fanny. Dickens visited her daily and paid for the best medical attention, but it was hopeless. She said, 'It was hard to die at such a time of life', he wrote to Forster; she felt sorry for her husband, Henry Burnett, 'going back to such a lonely home', and for her children, in particular one who was crippled. She died in September 1848, and was soon joined in her grave by her little crippled son.

Chapter Eighteen

Perfect Possession

HAVING COMPLETED *Dombey and Son*, DICKENS AGAIN LET NEARLY a year pass with no new novel begun. Apart from his Christmas story, he wrote only a few newspaper articles about the evils of poverty, ignorance, and other diseases afflicting the body of a country that seemed more concerned with imperial problems abroad. He was also still horrified by public hangings, and created a great stir and 'a roaring sea of correspondence' by writing two letters to *The Times* on the subject.

He started the Christmas story in October 1848, and had it written by the end of November, at the cost of a face so frowning that it 'utterly confounds and scares the House'. He worked every morning in his room, and would 'wander about the streets full of faces at night'. *The Haunted Man*, little less sentimental than *The Battle of Life* – Dickens finished it 'crying my eyes out' – was, like the earlier story, a working out of his own 'phantoms of past and present despondency'. Redlaw, a conventionally successful man, learns to accept and cherish his gnawing memories of past unhappy times, of suffering youth, lost love, negligent parents, a dead sister. The book sold as well as usual, and was staged by Mark Lemon, with some help from the author.

Dickens found his own lesson a hard one. In his restlessness he had started to examine his own springs closely, but all that he could feel was pity for himself and exoneration for the difficult man he had grown up to be. In an attempt to do as Redlaw does, come to terms with his sorrows, he started to write an autobiography, but was unable to go on when he reached his romance with Maria Beadnell. A different approach was required, an act of imagination, of symbolism, poetry.

Although preoccupied, he did not fail to enjoy Christmas with his family as much as ever. At Charley's Twelfth-Night birthday party, his daughters wanted him to dance the polka with them and had taught him the steps. The night before the party, lying in bed, he feared he might have forgotten them, and jumped on the cold floor to practise, solemnly. He told Forster the story, adding, 'Remember that for my biography.' With magic lantern and conjuring, he did his usual wonders for the children. An early biographer wrote:

Dickens's relations with children were ideal in character, and Miss Dickens recalled that he was a most kind, indulgent, and considerate father, always gentle to them about their small troubles and infantine terrors. She remembered how he would sing to them of an evening before bedtime, to their great delight, as, with one seated on his knee

160

Left: A montage showing Dickens with a group of his distinguished friends and contemporaries. Back: G. Macdonald, A. J. Froude, Wilkie Collins, Anthony Trollope. Front: W. M. Thackeray, Lord Macaulay, Lord Bulwer-Lytton, Thomas Carlyle, Charles Dickens

and the others grouped around, he would at their request go through no end of songs, mostly of a humorous kind, and laugh over them quite as much as his small listeners, enjoying them quite as much too.

The next day he was off to East Anglia on a quick holiday, but back in time for the birth on 15 January of his eighth child, Henry Fielding Dickens. At Broadstairs the previous summer Kate had been rattled in a chaise with a bolting pony; whether or not that was a reason, this birth was a difficult one. He helped her through it with chloroform, although 'the doctors were dead against it.... It spared her all pain ... and saved the child all mutilation.'

Soon Kate was quite well again and often entertaining guests at Devonshire Terrace. Jane Carlyle comments sharply on how one ate *chez* Dickens, in contrast to the simple tastes of the aristocracy: 'the profusion of figs, raisins, oranges, och! such overloaded dessert' – 'quantities of *artificial* flowers' – and the dishes 'served in the new fashion', not placed on the table but handed round by servants. Apart from the Carlyles, the guests at just one dinner party included Samuel Rogers ('who ought to have been buried long ago'), Thackeray, 'Phiz', Douglas Jerrold, Mrs Gaskell ('a natural unassuming woman, whom they have been doing their best to spoil by making a lioness of her'), the Unitarian minister Edward Tagart, and Mrs Tagart. Another visitor to the house (and Thespian), G.H. Lewes, remarked of Dickens, 'He remained completely outside philosophy, science, and the higher literature, and was too unaffected a man to pretend to feel any interest in them.' In conversation he was vivacious even on the most serious topics, a rare gift.

In February, at Brighton, Dickens lighted upon the title of the novel in which he would write the imaginary autobiography that preoccupied him. When Forster pointed out that the initials of *David Copperfield* were the author's own, reversed, Dickens was startled. Yet it was not the only example – there are Carker and Dombey, Clennam and Dorrit, Carton and Darnay, Marion and Grace, and a number of others – and in this of all his books it was an appropriate signal.

It is like a dream of his life, and works as a dream works, by dislocation, symbol, reversal, compression. The John Dickens who allowed his son to work in the blacking factory is isolated as the tyrannical stepfather Mr Murdstone; the prolix, improvident John Dickens is represented by Mr Micawber. The childlike Dora Spenlow whom David marries is the Maria who infatuated and jilted him; the married Dora comes to resemble Kate – 'There can be no disparity in marriage like unsuitability of mind and purpose', David reflects. His lost seraphic mother is the mother who irreversibly pulled down the heaven of childhood, when 'everything was happy ... the best and purest link between this world and a better', when she wished him back in the blacking factory. In the very tenderness of his sympathy with the child expelled, as he was, from Eden, washing bottles, one may detect a defence of his social aspirations, frustrated in the blacking factory, now fulfilled beyond dreams; a defence that elsewhere he expressed as a radical indignation that any child could be used so.

And so one could go on (and many have gone on), teasing out thread after thread,

Left: The frontispiece by Phiz to David Copperfield

and still the book will be, as any great poetic novel is, a tapestry that neither bio-graphical hindsight nor analysis can explain away. Dickens knew what he was at – 'I really think I have done it ingeniously and with a very complicated inter-weaving of truth and fiction' – and built that knowledge into the book by allowing David, in the first person, to be aware of the play of memory in the account he gives of his life. It served, for a while, to mend the broken places within his own memory, and always remained his own favourite among his novels. 'I can never approach the book with perfect composure', he wrote some years later, 'it had such perfect possession of me when I wrote it.'

From the first instalment, in May 1849, the book was a popular success. 'By jingo it's beautiful', Thackeray admitted, admiring 'those inimitable Dickens touches which make such a great man of him . . . there are little words and phrases in his books that are like personal benefits to his readers. . . . Bravo Dickens.' It was the first book Dostoevsky asked for when he was released from prison.

After a 'lumbering' start, the writing of it went on 'like a house afire', Dickens wrote to Forster from Broadstairs. A move to the Isle of Wight for a family holiday interrupted the flow, Dickens complaining of sickness, weakness, doziness and 'a disposition to shed tears from morning to night', but a move back to Broadstairs braced him.

Later episodes he wrote in London, Brighton, Paris, and back in Broadstairs. 'May it be as good a book as I hope it will be, for your children's children to read', he wrote to Macready; and to Forster, in October 1850, amid a final tide

Right: 'Mr Micawber delivers some valedictory remarks'. An illustration by Phiz for David Copperfield

BROADSTAIRS FROM THE CLIFF
1858.

Above: Broadstairs from the cliffs.

of 'tremendous' work and more ideas than he could use, 'I am within three pages of the shore; and am strangely divided, as usual in such cases, between sorrow and joy. Oh, my dear Forster, if I were to say half of what Copperfield makes me feel to-night, how strangely, even to you, I should be turned inside out! I seem to be sending some part of myself into the Shadowy World.'

Meanwhile in March 1850 a new weekly miscellany, *Household Words*, had started to appear, 'Conducted by Charles Dickens'. It was the fulfilment of the idea, then entitled *The Cricket*, from which, dissuaded by Forster, he had turned to the *Daily News* some years before. Of the new magazine, Dickens owned half (and paid himself £500 a year), the printers Bradbury and Evans owned a quarter, and the rest was split between Forster and the sub-editor W.H. Wills, a thin, sharp-nosed, experienced journalist whose efficient administration had been proved when he was Dickens's personal secretary at the *Daily News*. Also on the editorial staff were John Dickens and George Hogarth.

Dickens's first idea for the title had been *The Shadow*: 'a certain Shadow which may go into any place ... and be supposed to be cognisant of everything ... a sort of previously unthought of power going about ... the "Thing" at everybody's shoulder ... I want him to loom as a fanciful thing all over London; and to get

165

up a general notion of "What will the Shadow say about this, I wonder? ... Is the Shadow here?"' Forster dispelled the Shadow, which had the flavour of a kind of journalism that would not be in vogue until the twentieth century. It was Lord Northcliffe, long after Dickens's death, who called him the greatest magazine editor the world had seen. There are modern echoes, too, in Dickens's injunctions to his staff: 'Brighten it, brighten it, brighten it!'

Household Words might have served as a model for the trivialized *Tit-bits* that Northcliffe introduced half a century later. Into his magazine, Dickens crammed popular education, information, campaigns against social abuses, all mixed up with entertainment, fiction, sentiment and humour. Contributors were anonymous, but the controlling tone – minutely controlled by Dickens, selecting, altering, cutting – was a good-humoured reform: 'Let us all improve ourselves and all abandon something of our extreme opinions for the general harmony.' A story about an unhappy marriage was rejected, lest it arouse 'too painful emotions'. Reform was sharply demanded in the treatment of paupers, factory conditions, prisons, sanitation, jerry-building, agricultural wages, education, divorce, trade-unionism, prejudices and abuses of all sorts. Opinions were not advanced with any leading-article assumptions, however: an attack on working conditions in the mines is embodied in an account of the prehistoric formation of coal and the industrial techniques of extraction. The magazine carried popularized explanations of all kinds of scientific and technological discoveries, brief biographies of scores of historical figures, accounts of old and new books and works of art, reports from home and abroad of events, adventures, projects, skills, institutions – the where and what and how of the world, and often the why. Throughout, the attempt is made to 'brighten it', make it vividly interesting: a group of people 'formed *entirely* in their hours of leisure by Polytechnic Institutes would be an uncomfortable community', as Dickens remarked in an article in the opening number, praising cheap theatres as 'The Amusements of the People'.

Much of it makes fustian reading today, but in its own day, a more self-improving one, it appealed to an audience spread throughout the classes, at a time when perhaps three people in every four were literate. The first number is said to have sold one hundred thousand copies. A fortnight later, a monthly news-supplement was added, *The Household Narrative of Current Events*.

Dickens would arrive at eight o'clock in the morning, and stride up and down for three hours dictating, habitually combing his hair. He was remorseless in his editing of contributors' work, provoking complaints from Mrs Gaskell among others, but *Household Words* proved itself as training-ground for many young writers, of whom Wilkie Collins, G.A. Sala, George Meredith, Sheridan Le Fanu and Coventry Patmore are best remembered.

Chapter Nineteen

Anywhere But Where I Am

DICKENS WAS IN DEMAND TO MAKE PUBLIC SPEECHES, AND often they were about the broad social problems he was attacking in *Household Words*. Of particular concern to him, however, was his more personal interest in helping indigent authors and artists. The means he chose, as before, was the most enjoyable form of philanthropy he knew, a further round of benefit performances by his amateur Thespians. Acting a part, he said, 'has charms for me – I hardly know for how many wild reasons – so delightful, that I feel a loss of, oh! I can't say what exquisite foolery, when I lose a chance of being someone in voice, etc, not at all like myself.' With a ninth child, Dora Annie, now added to his dependants, and his newly-married brother Fred taking after his father by touching him for loans (which Dickens conceded, with stiff lectures), he might well wish to hide himself inside a costume.

The scheme this time was more ambitious than the earlier benefit work. With the dandified Edward Bulwer-Lytton, he proposed to set up and fund a Guild of Literature and Art, a provident society which would insure distinguished writers and artists against poverty, and house a group of them in cottages to be built for the purpose on Bulwer-Lytton's estate at Knebworth, in Hertfordshire. That few writers and artists, when they heard of the scheme, could slough off their surly independence and welcome the offered patronage, did not deter its sponsors. Bulwer-Lytton would write a costume comedy, *Not So Bad as We Seem*, and Dickens would produce it, starting with a performance for the Queen at the Duke of Devonshire's house in Piccadilly.

An added attraction for Dickens was that he would be able to act again with the Hon. Mary Boyle, a woman two years older than himself, whom he had met when visiting the Watsons, his friends from Lausanne, at Rockingham Castle, their place in Northamptonshire. He had danced and flirted and played a few dramatic scenes with her which had delighted the other guests and household staff. She had been unable to join Dickens's company at the end of 1850, when they played some farces at Knebworth to an aristocratic audience. Kate had been in that company until, with the clumsiness that Dickens laughed at, she fell through a trapdoor and sprained her ankle. Georgina was in the play too, and 'covered herself with glory'. Kate and Georgina, and Charley, home from Eton, acted in more farces in January 1851, at Rockingham, but now Mary Boyle had joined them, and quite stole the show.

After a brief holiday in Paris, Dickens started work on the play in February,

Opposite: Augustus Egg's portrait of Dickens as Sir Charles Coldstream in Used Up

168

with a reading of it to the cast by the great Macready, a week before his retirement from the professional stage (an event marked by a banquet that Dickens organized). Then Dickens plunged himself into the painstaking, exhausting labour of production that he loved. As well as all the usual details, there was a portable stage to be built, to facilitate the touring of the play. The royal performance was arranged for 30 April.

But it had to be postponed. Dickens was overtaken by distress in his family. First, the new baby was seriously ill, then Kate went down with symptoms suggestive of a nervous breakdown. She went to Malvern to recover, and while she was there John Dickens, after a 'terrible operation', died, 'O so quietly', on the last day of March. 'My poor father....' Unable to sleep, Dickens walked all night round the slums of London.

A fortnight later, Dickens spoke at a dinner of how an actor was obliged to go on stage and play a part even when he may just have witnessed 'scenes of sickness, of suffering, ay, even of death itself'. When he sat down, Forster and Lemon gave him a message that had arrived just before he started to speak. His baby daughter, with whom he had played that afternoon, had suddenly died in convulsions. Forster went to fetch Kate from Malvern, and Lemon shared Dickens's vigil by the body till morning.

The royal opening night was deferred until the middle of May. All the tickets, at five guineas, were sold. Certain precautions had been necessary: for one, a pipe could not be smoked on stage, since the Queen loathed tobacco, and even mock

Right: Tavistock House, The Dickenses' home from 1851–60

smoke made of cotton was prohibited, for 'Her Majesty would *think* she smelled tobacco.' At the end of the performance, the royal hands led the applause and, to the strains of the Duke's private band, the Queen sat in a garlanded chair to preside over a supper.

To the next performance, in the same ducal house a fortnight later, was added a short farce, largely improvised by Dickens and Lemon, in which the former played six parts. The show moved on to the Hanover Square Rooms for four enthusiastically received evenings, and later in the year toured to Bath ('a horribly dull audience') and Clifton ('prodigious'), and in 1852 to Manchester, Liverpool, Shrewsbury, Birmingham, Nottingham, Derby, Newcastle, Sunderland, Sheffield, and back to Manchester and Liverpool. The 'perfect army' of stage-staff and some thirty actors filled most of the hotels where they stayed. Playing sometimes to audiences of three thousand, the production made a profit for the Guild in the region of £5000.

All the time Dickens was assiduously conducting *Household Words*, in which his *Child's History of England* was appearing. He was also hunting for a larger house, and finally found it in Tavistock Square. At £1450 for a forty-five year lease, Tavistock House was 'decidedly cheap – most commodious – and might be made very handsome'. Reconstructed, refitted, redecorated, and refurnished, all exactly to Dickens's requirements, very handsome it soon was, and the family moved in at the end of November 1851, taking their garden shrubs with them from Devonshire Terrace.

While waiting to move in, Dickens experienced 'violent restlessness ... intolerable restlessness ... I sit down between whiles to think of a new story, and, as it begins to grow, such a torment of a desire to be anywhere but where I am ... takes hold of me, that it is like being *driven away*.' A few weeks later, 'I am wild to begin a new book, and can't until I'm settled.' Whether it was the move into the new surroundings, or whether *David Copperfield* had relaxed and concentrated his mind, the writing of *Bleak House*, the new book in monthly parts, proceeded with fewer cries of despair than usual once he had begun it. Yet it was a more complex work than any he had attempted before, representing the whole of society as an integrated structure, in which the acts of the highest and lowest are seen to have repercussions upon each other – seen by us, the readers, but not by the characters amid its swirling fog. Of the law, the central social institution, Dickens writes, 'The one great principle of the English law is, to make business for itself.' Within its fog, it has no perception of the society it is supposed to represent and serve. Exactly the same is true of Parliament, that 'Great Dust Heap'. Coodle and Doodle follow each other in and out of power in a charade that takes no notice of the common people, who are the victims of the exploitation that power foments when it is representative only of vested interests bound in leather tradition. Dickens had spent years of his young life watching both institutions at work, had since seen how the tentacles of injustice and greed spread throughout society, strangling warm hearts, and was now at the point where he found 'nothing in the present age at once so galling and so alarming to me as the alienation of the people from their own public affairs. . . . I know of nothing that can be done beyond keeping their wrongs continually before them.' What can't be endured must be cured.

From its first issue *Bleak House* sold about ten thousand copies more than *David Copperfield* had. 'I have never had so many readers', Dickens said, when he finished it in the autumn of 1853.

Kate, too, had been writing a book for Bradbury and Evans, entitled *What Shall We Have For Dinner? satisfactorily answered by numerous Bills of Fare for from two to eighteen persons.* The author was 'Lady Maria Clutterbuck', the wife of

Below: 'Friendly Behaviour of Mr Bucket'. An illustration by Phiz for Bleak House

'Sir Jonas Clutterbuck'. A few weeks after its publication, Kate gave birth to a tenth baby, Edward Bulwer Lytton Dickens. His father declined to be congratulated.

Left: An illustration by Phiz for the first edition of Bleak House *in 1853*

What strange kings those were in the Fairy times, who, with three thousand wives and four thousand seven hundred and fifty concubines found it necessary to offer up prayers in all the Temples for a prince as beautiful as the day! I have some idea, with only one wife and nothing particular in any other direction, of interceding with the Bishop of London to have a little service in Saint Paul's beseeching that I may be considered to have done enough towards my country's population.

One modest advantage of having so many children was that as the highlight of the annual Christmas festivities Dickens could coax and coach them all into a Twelfth-Night play of some ambition. At such an event at Tavistock House, Thackeray laughed so much that he rolled off his chair and lay weeping on the floor.

Bleak House was finished at Boulogne; in a château which Dickens rented for his family in the summer of 1853. The novel, the weekly magazine, his energetic help to Miss Coutts in the creation of a block of model flats and all his social engagements had exhausted him, and brought on a kidney spasm. 'I really feel as if my head would split like a fired shell if I remained here', he wrote from Tavistock House, and a brief spring holiday in Brighton was only a temporary palliative. From Boulogne, he went on firing continual letters across the Channel to Wills about *Household Words*, but was soon 'brown, well, robust, vigorous, open to fight any man in England of my weight, and growing a moustache' (which would shortly be joined by a beard).

Among the usual stream of visiting friends was Wilkie Collins, whose contributions to the magazine and acting in the theatricals had led to a lively friendship with Dickens, twelve years his senior. For some years the friendship with Forster had been cooling: Dickens needed the distraction of Collins's hedonistic clowning. A mild, raffish, spindle-shanked man, Collins was happy to accompany Dickens in any jaunt. In the autumn of 1853, together with the artist Augustus Leopold Egg, a morose foil to the boisterous spirits of the other two, Dickens and Collins set off on a two-month tour of Switzerland and Italy.

They visited many haunts and acquaintances of Dickens's previous visits, driven along by the dynamo of his energy, now released from the discipline of *Bleak House*. He even insisted on another ascent of Vesuvius, in company with Henry Layard, the archaeologist. Lately elected to Parliament, Layard had radical discussions in Italy with Dickens, who would two years later call him 'the most useful man in England'.

Dickens found the political situation in Italy as dilapidated as the gardens of the Palazzo Peschiere. Four years earlier he had admired the revolution in Rome; and when it was put down by Louis Napoleon had drafted the appeal for aid and political asylum in England for the refugees. The revolutionary leader Mazzini had dined at Devonshire Terrace, at a time when the Home Office was spying on him and censoring his letters. Now, in Italy, Dickens saw nothing but the dead hand of reaction.

Below: Wilkie Collins in 1858

Among the friends he visited were the de la Rues, in Genoa. Mme de la Rue still suffered from her nervous affliction, but declined Dickens's offer to renew his mesmeric treatment, which he had more recently practised successfully upon the artist John Leech. They both sent their warm regards to Kate, which Dickens,

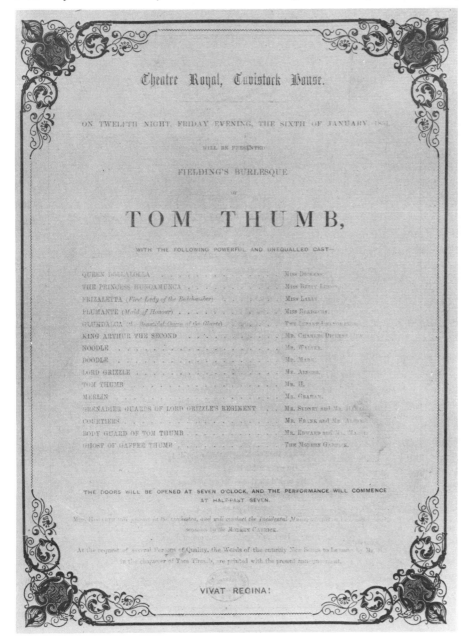

Left: Playbill for Henry Fielding's Tom Thumb *at Tavistock House in which Dickens, appearing as 'the modern Garrick', took the part of the Ghost of Gaffer Thumb*

in one of many affectionate, gossipy letters home, passed on, with the hope that Kate would reciprocate them. He reminded her of the embarrassment she had once put him in *vis-à-vis* Mme de la Rue, and asked her if now, in the perspective of time, she could not see the business for what it had truly been, an intense intellectual pursuit such as characterized him at many other times. 'Whatever made you unhappy in the Genoa time had no other root, beginning, middle, or end, than whatever has made you proud and honoured in your married life.... Now I am perfectly clear that your position beside these people ... is not worthy of you at all.' Kate did what he asked.

Travelling back through Paris, Dickens had arranged to meet his son Charley, who had left Eton and was in Leipzig studying German in preparation for a mercantile career. The Channel packet was late in to Dover, but the railway-station manager, knowing that Dickens was expected, 'detained train for London for distinguished author's arrival, rather to the exasperation of British public'.

For the next fortnight it was Christmas plays and parties. Among the entertainments were comic ballads sung by little Harry, at the age when his father had been praised for singing them. Immediately afterwards Dickens went to Birmingham with Kate and Georgina; there, for the first time, he was to give public readings from his books, for the benefit of the Birmingham and Midland Institute. It was a means of expressing his thanks for the reception he had been given in Birmingham a year earlier, when he spoke of the interest in literature among working men. 'From the shame of the purchased dedication, from the scurrilous and dirty work of Grub Street, from the dependent seat on sufferance at my Lord Duke's table today, and from the sponging-house or Marshalsea tomorrow ... the people have set literature free.' For three hours he read his *Christmas Carol* to an audience of two thousand in the Town Hall. Two days later he read *The Cricket on the Hearth*. Both audiences responded enthusiastically, but the best audience of all was the last, which at Dickens's request was comprised of working people at reduced ticket prices. Of the *Carol* they understood everything, he said, and responded to everything. 'I felt as if we were all bodily going up into the clouds together.' Invitations to read elsewhere poured in, but for the time being Dickens refused them.

He had other, urgent things on his mind. The circulation of *Household Words* was in decline, and the remedy was that Dickens would write a new novel in weekly numbers, a discipline to which he had not submitted himself since *Barnaby Rudge*, thirteen years earlier. An idea for the new work had already 'laid hold of me by the throat in a very violent manner'. It was to be that 'heaviest blow in my power' he had sworn to strike on behalf of the victims of factory and coal-mine.

Chapter Twenty

Through All This Time

AT THE END OF JANUARY 1854, DICKENS TRAVELLED TO PRESTON, where the cotton workers had been on strike for nearly half a year. He did not like the place, although he respected the orderly, democratic meetings of strikers that he witnessed. But before starting to write *Hard Times*, he wanted to observe for himself the reality of an industrial life ruled by materialistic laws of supply and demand, the system of high profits, cheap labour and cheaper lives that practised what the utilitarians preached as politico-economic orthodoxy.

Observed reality, in fact, the way people lived and felt and spoke in a place like Preston, is not strongly marked in the book. It is 'an analysis of Industrialism, rather than experience of it', as Raymond Williams says in *Culture and Society*. Bernard Shaw characterized the book as 'Karl Marx, Carlyle, Ruskin, Morris, Carpenter, rising up against civilization itself as a disease, and declaring that it is not our disorder but our order that is horrible; that it is not our criminals but our magnates that are robbing and murdering us.' Dickens's indignation has 'spread and deepened into a passionate revolt against the whole industrial order of the modern world'.

In what Shaw says lies another contradiction between Dickens the famous man and Dickens the writer. As tentatively in *Barnaby Rudge*, and more openly by the time of *Dombey and Son*, so now in *Hard Times* Dickens, who had recently told the Birmingham mechanics to join their masters in social reform, is declaring that reform is beside the point. The whole system is rotten. 'His positives do not lie in social improvement', Raymond Williams argues. 'It is not the model factory against the satanic mill ... it is, rather, individual persons against the system ... the Circus against Coketown.' The intuitive, generous, natural life of Sissy Jupe and the circus people is the only hope of salvation, and no amount of reform will admit those instincts into puritanical industrialism.

To produce such an argument in fictional form was an enormous challenge to Dickens and drove him 'three parts mad', crushed as it was into short weekly instalments. It is a brief book, scarcely a quarter the length of *Bleak House*, and was written by the middle of July, in under six months. It served its purpose – the circulation of *Household Words* was at least quadrupled, in spite of some readers' nervousness of the radical implications – but by the time he finished it, again at Boulogne with his family, Dickens felt 'used up'. It had left him very little time for sociable distractions, and now he felt 'as if nothing in the world, in the way of intense and violent rushing hither and thither, could quite restore my balance'.

Opposite: Industrial northern England in the latter part of the nineteenth century

At least his absorption in work had served to distract him from the quotidian state of affairs. When he looked up from his desk, what he saw was more intolerable than ever. With the Crimean War, declared in March 1854, the government could 'busy giddy minds with foreign quarrels', as Shakespeare put it. As an excuse for abdicating even the pretence of social improvement, it was swallowed as readily by the English people as by their rulers. Popular contributions to aid the war effort sickened Dickens. 'When I consider the Patriotic Fund on the one hand, and on the other the poverty and wretchedness engendered by cholera, of which in London alone, an infinitely larger number of English people than are likely to be slain in the whole Russian War have miserably and needlessly died – I feel as if the world had been pushed back five hundred years.' It was like the concern for heathen souls in the colonies that he had pilloried in *Bleak House*, seeing 'the old cannon-smoke and blood-mists obscure the wrongs and sufferings of the people at home'. Yet he was totally in favour of fighting the war: 'Russia MUST BE stopped.'

His predicament was frighteningly dramatized at Boulogne. When Prince Albert crossed the Channel to meet Louis Napoleon and review the French troops, Dickens patriotically hoisted the Union Jack and Tricolour over the haystack where, every day, he fell asleep in the sun, a book in his hand. Later, taking a walk along the Calais road, he met Albert and Louis Napoleon on horseback. They raised their hats to each other without speaking, Dickens noting that the Emperor was more stooping than in the old days at Gore House, before he had taken the throne. That night Dickens illuminated the house windows with a blaze of festive candles, at which his fervently Napoleonist landlord '*danced and screamed*' with joy. Dickens's own feelings towards the suppressor of the Italian revolution were much cooler. And his feelings about the domestic impact of the war were horrifyingly brought home to him when cholera struck his own family at Boulogne. Mary was desperately sick, and Dickens had to do what he could to treat her and isolate the other children. Fortunately, he was successful.

So vehemently did he write in *Household Words* against government inaction at home, and urge the workers – who had no vote – to unite with the middle class and throw the government out, that he alarmed many readers, including Miss Coutts. He did not like strikes, bread riots, looting, but he saw that the common people had no alternative voice. Why, the government could not even fight the war efficiently! Three-quarters of the Crimean army were dead of unmedicated wounds, disease, and frostbite. When Coodledeen resigned, he was succeeded by Doodleston. The country was riddled with rich sinecures, starting at Downing Street.

After two idle months since finishing *Hard Times*, relieved by twenty-mile walks, alone or with any friend who could be pressed, and by 'dreadful thoughts of getting away somewhere altogether by myself', he was back in London. At

Christmas he gave three more readings of his *Carol*, one of them, at the Bradford Mechanics' Institute, to an audience of nearly four thousand. There was the Twelfth-Night play to produce in the nursery, the cast augmented by Lemon, Collins, and the Inimitable. A week in Paris, a 'blaze of dissipation', was planned with Collins – anything to distract him from idleness, from sitting quietly in a room at home. But it was when he was sitting at home, after glancing at a few unopened letters, that he was visited by a very odd, reminiscent mood. He looked again at one of the envelopes and recognized, after more than twenty years, the handwriting of Maria Beadnell.

A few days previously, he had written to Forster: 'Why is it, that as with poor David, a sense always comes crushing upon me now, when I fall into low spirits, as of one happiness I have missed in life, and one friend and companion I have never made?' Now he opened her letter, he told Maria, 'with the touch of my young friend David Copperfield when he was in love'.

Right: Mrs Henry Louis Winter who as Maria Beadnell had been Dickens's first love. They met again in 1855 but Dickens was sadly disillusioned and embodies his impressions of her in Flora Finching in Little Dorrit

She had written to renew her friendship with a man now famous. He wrote back, at length, remembering a 'Spring in which I was either much more wise or much more foolish than I am now', in search of 'the changeless Past'. He was off to Paris, he told her, but as soon as he returned she must come with her husband, Henry Winter, to dinner. Perhaps he could buy something in Paris for her two small daughters? She replied that brooches would be very acceptable; he bought them, and also, for her, a choker ornamented with stones, blue stones. He had talked of her in Paris, he told her: Lady Olliffe had asked him if it were true 'that I used to love Maria Beadnell so very, very, very much? I told her there was no woman in the world, and there were very few men, who could ever imagine how much.' Had she seen that reflected in *David Copperfield*, and 'little bits' of herself in Dora?

People used to say to me how pretty all that was, and how elevated it was above the little foolish loves of very young men and women. But they little thought what reason I had to know it was true.... I have never been so happy a man since, as I was when you made me wretchedly happy: I shall never be half so good a fellow any more ... perhaps you have once or twice laid down that book, and thought, 'How dearly that boy must have loved me, and how vividly this man remembers it!'

She had asked him to write to her in confidence. He had done so, probably more confidentially than she had expected, attributing everything of passion and determination in himself to the idea of her, to the days of his life which 'had you for their Sun'. That Maria wrote back in kind can be deduced from his next letter:

Ah! Though it is so late to read in the old hand what I never read before, I have read it with great emotion.... How it all happened as it did, we shall never know this side of Time; but if you had ever told me then what you tell me now, I know myself well enough to be thoroughly assured that the simple truth and energy which were in my love would have overcome everything.

He could not believe that she was, as she said, 'toothless, fat, old and ugly'. Only recently he had walked along the old streets asking himself 'whether any reputation the world can bestow is repayment to a man for the loss of such a vision of his youth as mine. You ask me to treasure what you tell me, in my heart of hearts. O see what I have cherished there, through all this time and all these changes!'

Before that family dinner, Maria now asked, might he and she not meet alone? It was difficult, he replied, since he was so well-known, but were she to call at Tavistock House on a Sunday afternoon, asking first for Catherine, 'It is almost a positive certainty that there will be none here but I.'

They did meet, and the Past was not changeless, after all. The shock he received was cruelly transcribed in *Little Dorrit*: 'Flora, always tall, had grown to be very broad too, and short of breath; but that was not much. Flora, whom he had left a lily, had become a peony; but that was not much. Flora, who had seemed enchanting in all she said and thought, was diffuse and silly. That was much. Flora, who had been spoiled and artless long ago, was determined to be spoiled and artless now. That was a fatal blow.' And 'with a caricature of her girlish manner' this 'grotesque revival' in à derelict theatre at once adopted, on the strength of his letters, so intimate a tone with him that Dickens feared she supposed they were to elope, there and then. He was terrified. The ghost was out of control. He was losing 'my hold upon myself'. The scene could have given Oscar Wilde the idea for *The Picture of Dorian Gray*.

He was touched by her pathetic knowledge that he was disappointed, but after the dinner with her dull husband, and her sneezes that gave him her cold, she did not relent. Her letters provoked him to reply, 'You make me smile, when you picture to yourself how weak I might be.' She plied him with requests for another meeting, he returned increasingly pompous excuses about the 'waywardness of an author's mind'. She reproached him, and once he did call on her at home, with Kate. The dog Daphne was in the hall, stuffed.

Chapter Twenty-one

To Escape From Myself

THE NERVOUS TENSION OF THE WHOLE EPISODE WITH MARIA had to be drained off somehow. Theatricals and politics were the immediate resource. A novel would follow, though with more difficulties, false starts and agitated roamings than ever before.

The plays, 'a regular old-style melodrama' by Collins, entitled *The Lighthouse*, and a farce, were to be performed to a small audience at Tavistock House. The company included Collins, Egg, Lemon, Georgina, Mary and Katey. Dickens acted, directed and managed with his usual panache: always vigilant and firm, one of his actors noted, but never dictatorial. After four performances, there was a benefit evening at a private theatre in Kensington.

'Private theatricals' was the phrase that the Prime Minister, Palmerston, chose as a sneer aimed at political meetings organized by Henry Layard with Dickens's support. Layard had been to see the Crimean charnel-house for himself, and came back boiling at the incompetent bureaucracy which masqueraded as Government. Dickens backed Layard's campaign to the hilt in *Household Words*. When a motion of censure was defeated in the Commons, Layard appealed to the people at public meetings. Miss Coutts was anxious, again, that class was to be set against class. They already were, Dickens told her: it was the upper class 'who have put *their* class in opposition to the country', and it would not take much to ignite 'such a devil of a conflagration as never has been beheld' since the French Revolution.

To the anachronistic 'dandy insolence' of Palmerston, Dickens replied, speaking at 'the first political meeting I have ever attended':

The public theatricals which the noble Lord is so condescending as to manage are so intolerably bad, the machinery is so cumbrous, the parts so ill-distributed, the company so full of 'walking gentlemen', the managers have such large families, and are so bent upon putting those families into what is theatrically called 'first business' – not because of their aptitude for it, but because they *are* their families – that we find ourselves obliged to organize an opposition. We have seen the *Comedy of Errors* played so dismally like a tragedy that we really cannot bear it. We are therefore making bold to get up the *School of Reform*, and we hope, before the play is out, to improve that noble Lord by our performance very considerably. If he object that we have no right to improve him without his licence, we venture to claim that right in virtue of his orchestra, consisting of a very powerful piper, whom we always pay.

'The country is silent, gloomy,' he continued, 'England has never found an enemy one-twentieth part so potent to effect the misery and ruin of her noble defenders as she has been herself.' Understanding nothing of the 'general mind ... the machinery of government goes round and round and the people stand aloof, as if they left it to its last remaining function of destroying itself, when it has achieved the destruction of so much that was dear to them.'

In his new novel Dickens wanted to embody his bitter view of the condition of England. His first title was *Nobody's Fault*, denoting the nightmare of a corrupt bureaucracy. In the end, he called the book *Little Dorrit*, and the controlling metaphor was of an interminable, Piranesian prison, as fog and mechanism had been of the two previous books. The metaphor is centralized in the first prison that had impressed itself on his boy's mind, the Marshalsea, where William Dorrit's face, after twenty years, bears 'the reflected marks of the prison bars'.

Perhaps Dickens's difficulty in starting the book was that, through his political

Below: Plan for the serialization of Little Dorrit, *originally titled* Nobody's Fault

Opposite: Cartoon inspired by All the Year Round

activities, he was too close to the precise details of the condition. It took him some while to pull out, to allow reformist propositions to dwindle in perspective, and to achieve the great symbolic sweep of his mythology – 'a more seditious book than *Das Kapital*', said Bernard Shaw. In Folkestone for the summer of 1855, swarming up cliffs for relaxation, he wrote the first numbers, which, when they started their monthly appearance later in the year, at once set a new record sale for Dickens which did not flag.

While at Folkestone, he gave a benefit reading of *A Christmas Carol*, with seats at five shillings, threepence for working men. Then he crossed the Channel, leaving Kate and the children at Boulogne while he joined Georgina in Paris to look for an apartment for the winter. A place was found in the Champs Elysées, the furniture ritually reshuffled, and the family fetched.

His work was well-known in France (and Germany) by translations, and the great critic Taine acclaimed him while he was in Paris. Among many celebrities, Dickens met George Sand, who, he found, has 'nothing of the blue-stocking about her, except a little final way of settling all your opinions with hers'. Accompanied by Collins, he visited the *diableries* of night-time Paris, and walked off any hangover by circumnavigating the walls of the city. Paris was obsessed by feverish gambling on the stock market; Dickens saw some of the exorbitant luxury that successful speculators indulged in, and it contributed to his portrait of Merdle.

On one of several trips back to England, he read the *Carol* at Peterborough (taking the opportunity to see Mary Boyle at Rockingham) and at Sheffield, on both occasions donating the proceeds to the local Mechanics' Institutes. The end of the war had done nothing to open the path of reform. Layard was fighting a hopeless battle, it seemed. Dickens no longer believed, in any case, that universal suffrage would serve any real purpose. The common people, he felt with Carlyle, were not given the education to use votes wisely, nor did they apparently resent their situation, except in times of actual hardship. Art and letters were in no better case.

Nor, indeed, was his own house, at present occupied by what he now called the 'imbecility' of his wife's family. All they left him, whenever they stayed there, was dust, dirt, and unpaid bills. 'I find that the skeleton in my domestic closet is becoming a pretty big one', he hinted to Forster. Neither wife nor country could console his spirit; only his work could.

It is much better to go on and fret, than to stop and fret. As to repose – for some men there's no such thing in this life.... The old days – the old days! Shall I ever, I wonder, get the frame of mind back as it used to be then? ... However strange it is to be never at rest, and never satisfied, and ever trying after something that is never reached, and to be always laden with plot and plan and care and worry, how clear it is that it must be, and that one is driven by an irresistible might until the journey is worked out!

Overleaf: 'Many Happy Returns' by W. P. Frith, *1856*

But there was one event, at least, which consoled his state of mind, fulfilling a pattern of 'the old days'. Walking near Rochester with Wills he showed him Gad's Hill Place and recalled how his father had told him that if he grew up a successful man he might live in that house. That same night, at dinner, Wills sat next to Eliza Lynn, a contributor to *Household Words*, and they conversed about where Wills had been that day. Eliza Lynn knew Gad's Hill Place well; she had lived there as a child, was now the owner, and was of a mind to sell it. 'It is written that you were to have that house', Wills exclaimed to Dickens.

After negotiations, Dickens paid £1790 for the place, had it repaired, renovated and enlarged, and thought of renting it out or using it at weekends. But it was a 'plain and comfortable place', beautifully situated, not far from London, had its Shakespearean associations: and above all he was proud of the property. 'I used to look at it as a wonderful Mansion (which God knows it is not), when I was a very odd little child with the first faint shadows of all my books in my head – I suppose.' In 1857 the whole family was installed there for the summer, and, though he still had the lease of Tavistock House, Dickens began to think of Gad's Hill Place as a permanent home. It was there, the same summer, that he welcomed Hans Christian Andersen as a guest for a fortnight; the ingenuous Dane outstayed his welcome, wept on leaving, and was commemorated by the inscription, 'Hans Christian Andersen slept in this room for five weeks which seemed to the family ages.' A 'bony bore', the Dickens girls called him.

By now Dickens was in the throes of another theatrical production. The play, *The Frozen Deep*, was a highly melodramatic piece by Collins, derived from accounts of an expedition to the Arctic on which all had perished. In the spring of 1856 Dickens had begun to get excited about it, but was committed to another summer in Boulogne – a holiday visited by Mary Boyle, among other friends, but cut short by a fresh outbreak of cholera. In the autumn, while still writing *Little Dorrit*, he dived into the play, which was to be produced at Tavistock House. Friends and family (though not Kate) were cast, and rehearsed twice weekly for months. Dickens grew another beard for his leading part, which he practised on twenty-mile walks north of London, shouting all the way. He invented lighting effects, supervised the scenic sets of his regular designer Stanfield and another, William Telbin (neither would let the other set eyes on his own work), collaborated with Collins on the script, and fed and housed an 'ark' of technicians: 'a painter's shop in the school-room; a gas-fitter's shop all over the basement; a dress-maker's shop at the top of the house; a tailor's shop in my dressing-room'.

With a specially written overture, the play opened on Twelfth Night 1857 to an audience of about a hundred, including Mary Boyle, and was repeated three times in the following week. We have Charley's word for it that his father's death scene fetched tears and sobs from all present, including the actors, a condition from which they were rescued by a savoury farce as after-piece.

Opposite: The title page from a Danish edition of David Copperfield and other stories, *1888*

Dickens was not so easily rescued from his post-play depression. 'The theatre has disappeared, the house is restored to its usual conditions of order, the family are tranquil and domestic, dove-eyed peace is enthroned in this study, fire-eyed Radicalism in its master's breast.' Like all compulsively tidy people, he adored the disorder of creation.

A dinner at the *Household Words* office kept him cheerful hours past midnight; 'pigeon pie, collared red partridge, ham, roast fowls, and lobster salad', it was a modest meal by the standards of Kate's cookery book. His old friends were there, Macready, Stanfield, Maclise, and Forster, now engaged to be married, a betrothal that astonished everybody and had the effect of 'scrunching and squeezing' the lady in her dismay at what she had taken on. Forster, however, though still a trusted adviser, was not the close friend he had been: resenting Wills's influence on *Household Words*, he withdrew from the magazine, and was also jealous of Dickens's more boisterous friendship with Collins. The latter, now on the staff of the magazine, accompanied Dickens in escapades round the theatres, where they made a stir among the actresses. 'Any mad proposal you please', or 'any tremendous way of passing the night', or 'anything sufficiently in the style of Sybarite Rome in the days of its culminating voluptuousness' would, Dickens told Collins, 'find

Opposite top: Gad's Hill Place, the 'wonderful Mansion' of Dickens's childhood dream, acquired in 1857
Opposite bottom: The comfortable study at Gad's Hill

Below: Cast of 'The Frozen Deep', including Wilkie Collins (kneeling with head on hand) and daughter Kate

a wildly insane response.... I am your man.'

Then, in the summer of 1857, Douglas Jerrold died. A benefit performance for his family was essential, Dickens decided, ignoring the family's protestations that there was really no need for 'the hat being carried round'. A gallery in Regent Street was swiftly found and fitted with the revived set for *The Frozen Deep*. Dickens charged his company through fresh rehearsals and, although he now had a business manager, Arthur Smith, still concerned himself with such details as sitting in the box office and selling seats. Her Majesty must be invited. She replied that she was most eager to see the play, but did not wish to appear committed to all such invitations, so perhaps they would take it to Buckingham Palace? No, Dickens answered, he would not 'feel easy as to the social position' there of his daughters. Her Majesty understood, and travelled to Regent Street with Prince Albert, the King of the Belgians, and a few score of courtiers, all of them being so impressed by the tragedy that Victoria waived a custom and remained after midnight for the farce. Before it began, she requested Dickens's attendance on her. But he was in farce dress, and begged to be excused. She renewed her request. He renewed his excuse. 'My gracious sovereign' understood. 'I was mighty glad to think', Dickens remarked, 'that I had carried the point.'

And on it went: more performances to hysterical audiences of over two thousand, benefit readings of *A Christmas Carol* in July, and off to Manchester, reading, acting, drinking champagne. But in the Free Trade Hall professional actresses were required to project across that vastness. Mrs Ternan was engaged, and her talented daughters Maria and Ellen.

Right: Ellen Ternan and her sisters, Maria and Frances, whose association with the author began with the Manchester performances of The Frozen Deep

Maria had seen the play and was fearful that it might so move her, on stage, that she could not go on.

> She had to take my head up as I was dying, [Dickens wrote to Mrs Watson] and to put it in her lap, and give me her face to hold between my two hands. All of which I showed her elaborately (as Mary had done it before) that morning. When we came to that point at night, her tears fell down my face, down my beard (excuse my mentioning that hateful appendage), down my ragged dress – poured all over me like rain, so that it was as much as I could do to speak for them. I whispered to her, 'My dear child, it will be over in two minutes. Pray, compose yourself.' – 'It's no comfort to me that it will soon be over,' she answered. 'Oh it is so sad, it so dreadfully sad. Oh, don't die! Give me time, give me a little time. Don't take leave of me in this terrible way – pray, pray, pray!!' Whereupon Lemon, the softest hearted of men, began to cry too, and then they all went at it together.... And, if you had seen the poor little thing, when the Curtain fell, put in a chair behind it – with her mother and sister taking care of her – and your humble servant drying her eyes and administering Sherry ... and the people in front all blowing their noses, and our own people behind standing about in corners and getting themselves right again. .

As they had to, in order to play the farce, in which the younger Ternan daughter, eighteen-year-old Ellen, was the ward of an elderly gentleman, Dickens, who falls in love with her beauty. But that performance was nothing compared with the second one in Manchester, when Dickens, said Collins, 'literally electrified the audience'.

'Low spirits, low pulse, low voice, intense reaction', Dickens reported of himself a week later. Collins must go away somewhere with him, 'anywhere ... will you rattle your head and see if there is any pebble in it which we could wander away and play at marbles with? ... I want to escape from myself. For when I *do* start up and stare myself seedily in the face, as happens to be my case at present, my blankness is inconceivable – indescribable – my misery, amazing.' But to the maturer friend Forster, Dickens confessed that it was not himself he had to escape from. It was 'Poor Catherine'.

They were not made for each other, he wrote,

> ... and there is no help for it. It is not only that she makes me uneasy and unhappy, but that I make her so too – and much more so. She is exactly what you know, in the way of being amiable and complying; but we are strangely ill-assorted for the bond there is between us. God knows she would have been a thousand times happier if she had married another kind of man, and that her avoidance of this destiny would have been at least equally good for us both. I am often cut to the heart by thinking what a pity it is, for her own sake, that I ever fell in her way.... What is now befalling me I have seen steadily coming since the days you remember when Mary was born.

His artistic temperament, Dickens allowed, was partly to blame, 'a thousand un-certainties, caprices, and difficulties of disposition; but only one thing will alter

197

that, and that is, the end which alters everything. . . . Too late to say, put the curb on, and don't rush at hills – the wrong man to say it to. I have now no relief but in action.'

Relief could be found in the Lake District with Collins, in physical action so violent that Collins commented, 'A man who can do nothing by halves, appears to me to be a fearful man.' A kind of desperate escape was to be had at Doncaster racecourse, where Dickens, despising the whole business (although he watched the Derby every year at Epsom), made three random selections on St Leger day and saw them all romp home. But in the end he had to return to Tavistock House, to Kate and to what had already passed between them during the rehearsals for the Manchester performances. Kate had opened a parcel sent by a jeweller, and in it found a bracelet intended not for her but for fair-haired, blue-eyed Ellen Ternan.

Kate knew the plot of the farce, in which the elderly gentleman loads presents of jewellery on the young girl he loves. She knew how eagerly Ellen had sought to please the Manager in her rehearsals, had sat on the arm of his chair and joined him in duets at the piano. She was insulted, under her own roof, and told Dickens so. He, with a knightly devotion to the pure maidenhood of Ellen, answered that Kate's suspicions were repulsive. How could she so besmear him in the watchful eyes of his own daughters? He would not have it. She must demonstrate her confidence in him, and her acceptance that Ellen was innocent, by calling on the Ternans at their home.

Kate sat at her dressing-table and put on her bonnet, sobbing: for of course she was going to do as Dickens had bidden her. Katey, the same age as Ellen, heard her mother's sobs and went in to ask her what was wrong. 'Your father has asked me to go and see Ellen Ternan', Kate murmured. Her daughter stamped her foot. 'You shall not go.' Kate obeyed her husband, not her daughter.

Chapter Twenty-two

Before Heaven and Earth

THERE WAS NO TURNING BACK NOW. DICKENS WAS RESOLUTE; he would sleep in a bedroom apart from Kate's and have the connecting door boarded up. Thus would the irreversible change in their marriage be signified to both of them, though naturally the outside world would not know.

His close friends were a different matter. As he had written to Forster, so he told Miss Coutts of the 'insurmountable barrier' between himself and Kate. 'You know that I have many impulsive faults . . . but I am very patient and considerate at heart, and would have beaten out a path to a better journey's end than we have come to, if I could.' Her slow, clumsy ways affronted him. She was incompetent: Georgina and himself had to arrange and run the household between them.

> She does not – and she never did – care for the children, [he told Miss Coutts] and the children do not – and they never did – care for her. The little play that is acted in your Drawing-room is not the truth, and the less the children play it, the better for themselves, because they know it is not the truth. . . . Mary and Katey (whose dispositions are of the gentlest and most affectionate conceivable) harden into stone figures of girls when they can be got to go near her. . . . It is her misery to live in some fatal atmosphere which slays every one to whom she should be dearest.

And to Mme de la Rue he wrote in the same exaggerated vein, adding, 'What we should do, or what the girls would be, without Georgy, I cannot imagine. She is the active spirit of the house, and the children dote upon her. Enough of this. We put the Skeleton away in the cupboard, and very few people, comparatively, know of its existence.' Kate herself, he said, had more than once suggested they should separate, but he had insisted that 'in appearance' they must remain together, for the children's sake.

It is fruitless to ask what truth there was in all that. There is never one truth. Kate's clumsiness could have been endearing to another man: that it exasperated Dickens suggests an irritability which had roots elsewhere. Likewise her incompetence: quite possibly Dickens made her incompetent and clumsy, or appear to be so, by the masterful assertion in himself of the opposite qualities. Such behaviour is seldom deliberate. What was deliberate, and cruel, was his refusal to imagine that Kate's relationship with her children might have had quiet depths of understanding to which he, in his more extravert parenthood, was a stranger. Katey certainly knew what truth she saw in it all: 'My father did not understand women.'

Unquestionably Kate was cowed by her famous and brilliant husband. She could not live up to his wit, grace, charm, energy. Few could. But she need not have suffered as a result, had Dickens not tormented her with her shortcomings and mocked them by his gallant flirtations with other women, who, known only superficially, idealistically, could not fail to shine in comparison. Dickens acknowledged his infantile fantasies when he wrote to Mrs Watson:

Left: Mrs Kate Dickens, increasingly dominated and disliked by her dynamic husband, both unhappy partners in a failing marriage

Realities and idealities are always comparing themselves before me, and I don't like the Realities except when they are unattainable – then, I like them of all things. I wish I had been born in the days of Ogres and Dragon-guarded Castles. I wish an Ogre with seven heads (and no particular evidence of brains in the whole of them) had taken the Princess whom I adore – you have no idea how intensely I love her! – to his stronghold on the top of a high series of mountains, and there tied her up by the hair. Nothing would suit me half so well this day, as climbing after her, sword in hand, and either winning her or being killed – *There's* a frame of mind for you, in 1857.

That letter testifies, as well as any of Dickens's admissions do, to the connection between his imaginative life, in which the magnificent metaphors of his novels were created, and the breakdown of something as mundane (to him, as to many) as a twenty-one-year marriage. In it is all the pathetic ambiguity of the word 'Romantic'. No young woman, if she is wise, should marry a writer who might turn into a great one.

The divided house was a gloomy one. Walter had already left it and gone to India as a military cadet: saying farewell to him had been like having 'great teeth drawn with a wrench' for Dickens. Twelfth Night was a silent night in 1858. Dickens found some distraction for his ennui in a round of charitable work, speaking, reading on behalf of poor schools and hospitals for sick children, attacking the wastefulness of the Royal Literary Fund. More often than ever, with the expense of buying Gad's Hill Place, he revolved the idea of doing for his own benefit what he had so successfully done for others, public readings from his books. Forster told him it would be vulgar. Dickens disagreed: apart from the profit, he relished the live contact with an audience. It would, at least, be something to do, while he was unsure about starting a new book. 'If I can discipline my thoughts into the channel of a story, I have made up my mind to get to work on one. . . . Sometimes, I think I may continue to work; sometimes, I think not. . . . Nothing whatever will do me the least "good" in the way of shaking off the one strong possession of change impending over us that every day makes stronger.' Later, he was more resigned to the 'circumstances at home. Nothing can put *them* right, until we are all dead and buried and risen. It is not, with me, a matter of will, or trial, or sufferance, or good humour, or making the best of it, or making the worst of it, any longer. It is all despairingly over. Have no lingering hope of, or for, me in this association. A dismal failure has to be borne, and there an end.' With the resignation came a greater disinclination to write. He told Collins, 'The domestic unhappiness remains so strong upon me that I can't write, and (waking) can't rest, one minute. I have never known a moment's peace, or content, since the last night of *The Frozen Deep.* . . . I have a turning notion that the mere physical effort and change of the Readings would be good.' What finally persuaded him was Miss Coutts's approval of the project.

With Arthur Smith as his business manager, Dickens mapped out a series of

Opposite: A bearded, middle-aged Dickens giving one of his extremely popular public readings, 1861

readings, starting in London and continuing all over the country. There were to be some three dozen appearances within a period of six months. Later he might go to Ireland, and even to America, where he supposed he might profit by as much as £10,000.

The series began on 29 April at St Martin's Hall, and the response and demand for tickets was so intense that the planned six readings in London were at once increased to sixteen. To *A Christmas Carol*, which he had often read at benefit occasions, Dickens added *The Chimes*, and later rehearsed further programmes including the death of Paul Dombey, some in-character Mrs Gamp scenes from *Martin Chuzzlewit*, and scenes from *Pickwick*.

Before the London series was completed, the ice wall at Tavistock House decisively crashed and broke. It was Kate's family who triggered it. The Hogarths, in Dickens's eyes, had already so come to resemble a pack of ungrateful jackals that he had once walked to Gad's Hill, thirty miles through the night, rather than stay at Tavistock House where they were. Mrs Hogarth, to whom Kate had confided all her troubles, had no doubt what must be done: leave him. And Kate did as her mother said.

The trouble was that her sister Georgina saw things quite differently. She was not going to leave her brother-in-law, for the sake of whose company she had once refused Egg's proposal of marriage. Georgina, possessing a 'remarkable capacity' as well as 'being one of the most amiable and affectionate of girls', was going to stand by Dickens after sixteen years, and how would that look to the world? At best, it would blunt the Hogarths' blade of accusation, at worst, give rise (as it did) to new scandal, which Dickens tried to pre-empt by going to lodge in his office at *Household Words*. Appearances, after all, must be kept up. He hoped, indeed, that the whole separation could be smoothed over, for what would the readers of, say, *Household Words* think if the conductor were repudiated by his wife? He would be generous in providing for Kate; would she accommodate his difficulties as a public man?

Forster was charged to negotiate a settlement for Dickens, Lemon represented Kate. They came up with propositions to save face. Kate might have her own rooms at Tavistock House and be the hostess when occasion demanded. Or Kate might consent to shuttle from Gad's Hill Place to Tavistock House in alternation with Dickens, like Mrs Fair Weather and Mr Foul. No, said Kate through her tears, it was better to separate completely. Her family agreed. So, resignedly, did Dickens. It was agreed that Kate should live in another house with a settlement of £600 a year. Charley was asked if he would join his mother there, and agreed that it was his duty, although he would miss his father and the other children at home – normally Mary, Katey, and the two smallest, since Walter was in India, and Frank, Alfred and Sydney were usually away at boarding-school in Boulogne.

And so it would have rested, but for the still unappeased fury of the Hogarths, chiefly Mrs Hogarth and her youngest daughter, twenty-five-year-old Helen. They let slip the word that Ellen Ternan was Dickens's mistress. It was a word that stained Ellen's purity, impugned Dickens's truthfulness, risked the reputation of his children, and it turned him, Katey said, into 'a madman. This affair brought out all that was worst – all that was weakest in him. He did not care a damn what happened to any of us.' But he was a madman with a will of steel tempered on tougher anvils than the Hogarth family. Not a penny, he said, for Kate, until publicly and fully, in writing, they retracted their gossip. He drew up the document for them himself. They would not sign it, they said. Oh yes they would, he answered. They spoke of taking him to court. Let them, he said.

The whole story was small-talk for the literary town by now. Thackeray threw his stick on the fire when, being told that it was all caused by an affair Dickens had with Georgina, he denied it: 'It's with an actress', he said, thinking that was less scandalous. For his pains, he received a livid letter from Dickens. Miss Coutts, acting as an intermediary for Kate, perhaps hinted at the thought of a reconciliation. It was of course out of the question: 'the weak hand that could never help or serve my name in the least, has struck at it – in conjunction with the wickedest people, whom I have loaded with benefits!'

'... we solemnly declare that we now disbelieve such statements.' After two weeks, the Hogarths did what Dickens told them to do, they signed the retraction. That ought to have been an end to it, sad, calumnious, but still a relatively private carnage. Dickens's pride was still aflame, however, imagining scandalous smirks in every parlour. Only a public statement could suffice. One after another, his friends told him to let it rest; very well, he conceded, he would take the advice of Delane, editor of *The Times*. Delane agreed with Dickens: publish the statement. Having first let Kate have a sight of it – she raised no objection – Dickens published it on the front page of *Household Words*. It explained that his long friendship with the public compelled him to share with them the truth behind any malicious gossip they might have heard. 'Some domestic trouble of mine, of long standing', had 'been brought to an arrangement' satisfactory to all concerned, but, by some means, 'misrepresentations, most grossly false, most monstrous, and most cruel – involving, not only me, but innocent persons dear to my heart' had been circulating.

I most solemnly declare, then – and this I do both in my own name and in my wife's name – that all the lately whispered rumours touching the trouble at which I have glanced, are abominably false. And that whosoever repeats one of them after this denial, will lie as wilfully and as foully as it is possible for any false witness to lie, before Heaven and earth.

He wanted all the newspapers to reprint the statement, and he cut Mark Lemon dead when that editor of *Punch* thought a humorous magazine an inappropriate place for it. Nothing so breeds a scandal as the denial of it, and soon readers all over England, egged on by the newspapers' own editorial remarks next to the statement, were gossiping about Dickens's affairs.

By now, Katey said in later life, 'nothing could surpass the misery and unhappiness of our home'. And still Dickens blundered on, deeper and deeper. As an extra precaution against malice he prepared a second, more explicit statement, which was to be shown only confidentially to genuine enquirers. Inevitably, it leaked out, and the press made hay of a man who thought so 'little of the marriage tie'. For Dickens now gave credit to Georgina for holding the home together. 'Some peculiarity' of Mrs Dickens's character had 'thrown all the children on someone else'. Through a 'mental disorder' Mrs Dickens 'felt herself unfit for the life she had to lead as my wife', but Georgina had for years striven to prevent a separation. The statement went on to assail those who had besmeared the name – not given – of 'a young lady' who was as 'virtuous and spotless', 'innocent and pure, and as good as my own dear daughters. . . . I am quite sure that Mrs Dickens, having received this assurance from me, must now believe it . . . in the perfect confidence I know her, in her better moments, to repose in my truthfulness.' Dickens was, of course, 'shocked and distressed' that the statement had been published, and self-righteously told Kate so. She, who had said almost nothing throughout the collapse of her home and marriage, did not raise her voice now.

Chapter Twenty-three

An Irresistible Night

THE SCANDAL DID NOT DETER DICKENS FROM CONTINUING WITH his readings, nor did it sour the enthusiasm with which they were received. On the contrary, the cheers that greeted him were warmer than ever, in loyalty or in admiration of the calm self-control of the man standing on at the lectern waiting for silence. As for the applause at the end, that was given in token of a versatility as arresting as the one-man plays of Charles Mathews he had watched as a young man. It was not achieved without many long hours of preparation in his study, where he cut and shaped the excerpts dramatically, found voices and gestures for dozens of characters, and wrote stage directions for himself in the margins: 'Rising action', 'Snap your fingers', 'Cupboard action' and so on. After some experience, he came to know the scenes by heart, and allowed himself to ad-lib when the mood took him. The only thing that could ever shake his self-control was when someone in the audience was so helpless with laughter that he infected Dickens.

Up and down and across England he read, and in Ireland and Scotland, sometimes to an audience of over two thousand, crushed against the platform. In all, he had given eighty-seven readings by the middle of November, and showed a clear profit of over £3000. He was, above all, a performing artist, and the warmth and gratitude that he evoked everywhere would be a wonderful reassurance to any writer's solitude, still more to Dickens when he was most in need of it after the break with Kate and the hounding by the press. 'I consider it', he acknowledged, 'a remarkable instance of good fortune that it should have fallen out that I should, in this autumn of all others, have come face to face with so many multitudes.' And to Mary Boyle, who arranged for a geranium to be ready for his buttonhole wherever he read, 'I hope I may report', he wrote, 'that I am calming down again. I have been exquisitely distressed.'

During his rest periods in London, the bitter spring still reverberated in quarrels. The most enduring was with Bradbury and Evans, who had been his publishers for fourteen years. Convinced that Evans had sided with the Hogarths, he forbade his family to speak to Evans, and instructed Forster to make arrangements that would sever the publishing contracts. Dickens would return to Chapman and Hall.

Against all the experience that Dickens and Forster had of hacking off unfavoured publishers like ivy, Bradbury and Evans stood no chance. The only ground on which they resisted was *Household Words*, refusing to sell their minority shareholding. Very well, Dickens would simply start a new weekly magazine, taking with him the best of the *Household Words* contributors. What shards of the magazine remained were useless to the printers, since Dickens, as the majority shareholder, could veto new appointments. Bradbury and Evans took the argument to court, but their case was hopeless and they were obliged to put their share to auction. By somewhat shady methods at the auction, Dickens acquired the rest of the property, and reckoned that it cost him no more than £500 after everything was settled.

By now, however, he had already begun publication of the new magazine, so incorporated the title of *Household Words* in it. His first suggestion for the new title had, as Forster pointed out, been bizarrely naive: *Household Harmony*. The final choice was *All The Year Round*. Dickens owned three-quarters of the property, Wills the other quarter. Together they quickly set to establishing the new business, and the first issue was dated 30 April 1859.

Each issue was led by an instalment of a serial story, of which the author was named. In other respects, it differed little from its predecessor: but this change was a shrewd one. Within a month, *All The Year Round* was selling three times as many copies as *Household Words* had, and by the end of Dickens's life its circula-

Below: A poster for a Dickens public reading

MR. CHARLES DICKENS
WILL READ IN THE ROUND ROOM, ROTUNDA, DUBLIN:—
On MONDAY EVENING, AUGUST 23rd, at 8 o'Clock, his
CHRISTMAS CAROL.
On TUESDAY EVENING, AUGUST 24th, at 8 o'Clock, his
CHIMES.
On WEDNESDAY AFTERNOON, AUGUST 25th, at 3 o'Clock, the Story of
LITTLE DOMBEY.
On THURSDAY EVENING, AUGUST 26th, at 8 o'Clock,
THE POOR TRAVELLER,
BOOTS AT THE HOLLY TREE INN· AND MRS. GAMP.
PLACES FOR EACH READING:—Stalls (numbered and reserved) Shillings; Unr Seats, Half-a-Crown; Back Seats, One Shilling.
Tickets to be had of Messrs. McGlashan and Gill, Publishers, &c., 50, Upper Street, Dublin, where a Plan of the Stalls may be seen.
Each Reading will last two hours.
☞ On only one occasion, during Mr. Dickens's experience, some ladies and gentlemen in the Stalls caused great inconvenience and confusion (no doubt, unintentionally), by leaving their places during the last quarter of an hour of the Reading, when the general attention could least bear to be disturbed. This elicited a strong disposition in other parts of the Hall towards an angry but not unreasonable protest.
In case any portion of the company should be under the necessity of leaving before the close of the Reading in the apprehension of losing railway trains, they are respectfully entreated as an act of consideration and courtesy towards the remainder, to avail themselves of the opportunity afforded by the interval between the parts when Mr. Dickens retires for five minutes.
[P. T. O.

tion, at 300,000, was around eight times higher than the earlier magazine at its peak.

The story serialized in the first six months was *A Tale of Two Cities*. Dickens made an innovation by publishing the same story simultaneously in monthly parts from Chapman and Hall. Making a start was difficult, as usual. Dickens used Carlyle's *History of the French Revolution* as his reference, but asked Carlyle if he could suggest any further background reading. Two cartloads of books were

Right: An illustration by Phiz for A Tale of Two Cities, *the last novel on which Dickens collaborated with this illustrator*

sarcastically delivered from the London Library. The finished work won Carlyle's approval, however. The weekly-instalment form was as taxing as ever. 'Nothing but the interest of the subject, and the pleasure of striving with the difficulty of the forms of treatment, nothing in the mere way of money, I mean, could also repay the time and trouble of the incessant condensation', the aptitude for which Dickens called 'a strange knack or lottery' to a contributor who did not possess it. George Eliot refused even to try it.

In dealing with a revolutionary mob, Dickens was more sympathetic than he had felt able to be in *Barnaby Rudge*. After all, it was only four years since he had predicted for his own country, if upper-class oppression continued, 'a devil of a conflagration'. As to the themes of love and sacrifice that sweep through the book, they must have aroused satisfying echoes in him of the experiences he had been through since Maria Ternan's tears had washed his tragic face in *The Frozen Deep*, while her sister Ellen watched from the wings. 'He dramatized himself both in fact and in fiction', his biographer Hesketh Pearson observes.

Dickens now spent much of his time in the company of people considerably younger than himself: Ellen Ternan, the children and Georgina at home, and the contributors to *All The Year Round*, who were known collectively as 'Dickens's Young Men'. For the last twenty years of his life he worked hard at his editorial job every week, reading manuscripts, cutting, trimming and rewriting them, corresponding with old and new contributors, but 'the Chief', as he was known, always had time to help young writers of promise. With Collins's early work he 'took unheard-of pains ... went over them line by line'. R. H. Horne, who had worked for *Household Words*, wrote that the Chief's

> conversation is genial. He hates argument; in fact, he is unable to argue – a common case with impulsive characters who see the whole, and feel it crowding and struggling at once for immediate utterance. He never talks for effect, but for the truth or for the fun of the thing. ... His sympathies are of the broadest, and his literary tastes appreciate all excellence. He is a great admirer of the poetry of Tennyson.

Another said that 'the very vehemence of his cheery good humour rather bore one down.' One of the 'young men', Edmund Yates, son of the actor Frederick Yates, wrote:

> I have heard Dickens described by those who knew him as aggressive, imperious, and intolerant, and I can comprehend the accusation; but to me his temper was always of the sweetest and kindest. He would, I doubt not, have been easily bored, and would not have scrupled to show it; but he never ran the risk. He was imperious in the sense that his life was conducted on the *sic volo sic jubeo* principle, and that everything gave way before him. The society in which he mixed, the hours which he kept, the opinions which he held, his likes and dislikes, his ideas of what should or should not be, were all settled by himself, not merely for himself, but for all those brought into connection with him, and it was never imagined they could be called in question. Yet he was never regarded as a tyrant; he had immense power of will, absolute mesmeric force, as he proved beneficially more than once.

Edmund Yates it was who triggered another quarrel in London, when he wrote a sneering article about Thackeray. The Committee of the Garrick Club, to which both of them (and Dickens) belonged, was embroiled in the row that ensued. In his break-up with Kate, Dickens had been defended by Yates and offended by Thackeray; while not approving of Yates's behaviour, Dickens therefore felt obliged to give him some support. When Thackeray learned that, he at once concluded that the whole incident had been instigated by Dickens as a revenge, and in consequence they were not on speaking terms for several years. Dickens's private view of the quarrel at the Garrick Club was, 'Upon my soul, when I picture them in that back-yard, conceiving that they shake the earth, I fall into fits of laughter which make my daughters laugh – away at Gad's Hill – until the tears run down their cheeks.'

A nastier episode concerned the Ternan family. Very little reliable evidence exists about Dickens's relationship with Ellen Ternan, but it is certain that he was a benefactor to the whole family. The oldest sister, with his help, had gone to Italy, accompanied by her mother, to study music, leaving Maria and Ellen on their own in Oxford Street, waiting for occasional work on the stage. Dickens learned that a policeman had been pestering them with questions about their home life, and he strongly suspected that the man 'has been surborned to find out all about their domesticity by some "Swell" ' – Dickens's rage was, of course, heated by the thought that he might himself be responsible, involuntarily, for any assumption that the Ternan girls were of easy virtue.

His own family concerned him a good deal. Charley seemed to be doing well enough in business, and Walter had proved himself as an officer in the Indian Mutiny, but the third son, Frank, a nervous boy, hovered between medicine and colonial farming. Dickens thought of a career in the Foreign Office for him, but for a while he was given a job at the magazine office. Alfred and Sydney, both still at school, were hoping to enter, respectively, the Army and the Navy. Sydney became a naval cadet; his sextant, Dickens affectionately remarked, 'on being applied to his eye, entirely concealed him' (Sydney was a very small boy). 'Not the faintest trace of the distinguished officer behind it was perceptible.' The two youngest boys were at Rochester Grammar School.

Mary, who was twenty when the marriage broke up, and Katey, a year younger, were more serious problems. The separation affected them quite differently. Mary was devoted to her father, and did not see her mother again until after Dickens was dead. Because her father disapproved of the man, she refused a proposal of marriage, and was depressed as a result. Katey, though she loved him, matched her father's spirit. She suspected that Georgina (who did not speak to her sister for twenty-one years, until Kate was on her deathbed) had been 'not quite straight' in the separation, and she implicitly reproached both Dickens and Georgina by regularly going to see her mother. In a similar spirit, and to escape the unhappy atmosphere at Gad's Hill Place, she defied her father and married Wilkie Collins's brother Charles, a pre-Raphaelite painter. Dickens knew Charles Collins from a short holiday they spent together at Broadstairs (what ghosts of summers past must have risen), and disapproved of the match with a man twelve years older than Katey, whom he guessed she did not love. After the wedding, to which Kate was not invited, Mary found her father weeping in Katey's empty bedroom, his head on her wedding-dress. 'But for me', he said through his tears, 'Katey would not have left home.'

Dickens's brothers were no consolation. Fred had turned up at a reading in Belfast, his marriage to Anna Weller near collapse (as Dickens had foreseen). He wanted to borrow money, naturally, and, after being 'dreadfully hard' with him, Dickens relented. Augustus was also asking his famous brother for help, from America, where he had gone after deserting his wife, for whom Dickens had to provide. A third brother, Alfred Lamert, had died, leaving a widow and five children dependent. The whole picture was summarized by Dickens: 'My mother, who was also left to me when my father died (I never had anything left to me but relations), is in the strangest state of mind from senile decay; and the impossibility of getting her to understand what is the matter, combined with her desire to be got up in sables like a female Hamlet, illumines the dreary scene with a ghastly absurdity that is the chief relief I can find in it.' He called on his mother when she was ailing, one day; 'the instant she saw me, she plucked up a spirit, and asked me for "a pound"'. As a final irony Maria Winter, whose parents had prevailed upon her thirty years before to marry a young man of more substance than Dickens, was now asking him for help, her husband's business having failed. Dickens courteously recommended that her father (who had refused to help, though a few years later he left an estate of £40,000) 'might be induced to do what – I may say to you, Maria – it is no great stretch of sentiment to call his duty.'

In several senses he was relieved when he decided to sell Tavistock House with all its opulent fittings, and all its memories, too. As a London *pied-à-terre* he furnished some rooms at the magazine offices. Seized with the desire to be clear of the past, he made a great bonfire at Gad's Hill of all the letters he had accumulated, thousands of them from celebrated figures who were now dying off. His two small sons 'roasted onions in the ashes of the great'. He had been 'shocked', Dickens said, 'by the misuse of the private letters of public men. Would to God every letter I had ever written was on that pile!'

One memorial of himself he did allow at this time was a new portrait (there had been many earlier ones) by W. P. Frith. Forster, who had commissioned the portrait just before *The Frozen Deep*, told Frith to wait until the 'whim' of a moustache had passed. Instead, for the play, Dickens grew a full door-knocker beard, and kept it.

Talking to his sitter, Frith, who deeply admired Dickens, told him that he was surprised at the 'sneaking' tone he adopted for Sam Weller in his readings. Dickens just nodded. A few days later, Frith heard from a friend that Weller's speeches the previous night were 'like pistol-shots'. Dickens confessed, 'I altered it a little – made it smarter.' Frith, a diffident man, expressed his amazement that any advice

214

of his could influence Dickens. 'On the contrary', Dickens smiled, 'whenever I am wrong I am obliged to anyone who will tell me of it; but up to the present I have never been wrong.'

There had been another series of readings in London in early 1859, and a further series in the Midlands at the end of the year, after *A Tale of Two Cities* had been completed. Then Dickens rested for a while, refreshing himself now and then with a trip to the seaside, and writing only the magazine essays later collected in *The Uncommercial Traveller*. Their content was often personal reminiscence, and one of them, he told Forster in September 1860, 'so opens out before me' that he had decided to abandon it as an essay and instead let it grow into a new serial story. He was forced to start writing it sooner than he expected: after Wilkie Collins's serial *The Woman in White* had finished, the circulation of the magazine declined rapidly, and, once more in his life, Dickens saved the situation with a story in weekly parts, beginning in December. *Great Expectations* 'will be written in the first person throughout, and ... you will find the hero to be a boy-child, like David', he wrote to Forster. 'To be sure I had fallen into no unconscious repetitions, I read *David Copperfield* again the other day, and was affected by it to a degree you would hardly believe.'

Dickens's unease at the social aspirations of the blacking-factory boy he had been, only hinted at in *David Copperfield*, swelled as the main theme now. Although the events in *Great Expectations* are not literally autobiographical, Pip's snobbishness cannot be isolated from the contrast in Dickens's own life between the factory and Gore House, the lifelong concern with social deprivation and the enjoyment of luxurious living. That is the sense in which, as Edgar Johnson says, the novel 'pierces fathoms down in self-understanding ... is relentless in self-judgment', and devoid of the self-pity of the earlier first-person book.

For Dickens, though free of his unhappy marriage, was still plagued by the old scars and toxins. The image of prison shadows this book again. Whatever he and Ellen Ternan were to each other, he was not cured of his restless anxiety, which writing, readings, and daily long walks, only temporarily eased.

Chapter Twenty-four

One Friend and Companion

FOR THE FIRST HALF OF 1861, DICKENS RENTED A HOUSE NEAR Regent's Park. The Ternan family were living not far away, and he spent some evenings at their house, playing cards and singing duets with Ellen. In the spring he gave six more readings in London. He was chiefly busy with finishing *Great Expectations*, which he did by June. The story was to have ended with Pip and Estella going their separate ways, but Dickens allowed Bulwer-Lytton to persuade him into a happier close.

The summer was spent at Gad's Hill. Over the years Dickens made many improvements to the house, 'as pleasantly irregular, and as violently opposed to all architectural ideas, as the most hopeful man could possibly desire'. Across the Dover Road was a shrubbery he had bought with the property; he had a tunnel built to it, under the busy road, and a few years later chose the shrubbery as the site on which to erect a Swiss chalet. An extraordinary present to him from a French actor, Charles Fechter, whom he admired and assisted, the chalet arrived, without notice, in ninety-four boxed pieces. When it had been assembled, Dickens made the upper room his study, among the treetops.

Gad's Hill Place itself was comfortably but not ostentatiously furnished. Dickens was usually surrounded there by his friends and family. After working in the morning, he would lead a twelve-mile walk through the countryside after lunch, taking some of his platoon of dogs – St Bernard, Irish bloodhound, mastiff, Newfoundland – who at other times were chained by the gate to deter tramps. After the walk there were very competitive games of rounders, cricket, battledore, croquet, bowling, and quoits. In his meadow a local working men's cricket team had permission to play, and every Christmas he organized the same men into holding a sports day. At dinner Dickens was a fount of laughter, not so much at his own stories as at what he egged on his guests to say: he 'invariably drew out what was best and most characteristic in others', Mary Boyle said. After dinner there were dances, and the games Dickens loved and shone at, charades and memory tests. Once, requiring an item to add to a memory-list, he said 'Warren's Blacking, 30, Strand', and would not explain it. There was punch to drink, which he enjoyed making but sipped abstemiously, and billiards before bedtime at midnight.

The family party at Gad's Hill at Christmas 1862 included Katey and Charles Collins, Charley and his wife Elizabeth, and their daughter Mary, Dickens's first grandchild. He had not attended the wedding, for Elizabeth's father was Frederick Evans, the printer with whom he had broken. He not only disapproved of the marriage, but also earnestly requested his old friend Thomas Beard 'not to enter Mr Evans's house' after the wedding, although Beard was Charley's godfather.

Charley himself was not doing well in his business career, showing disturbing signs of his grandfather's imprudence. Frank was still more of a problem. At the *All The Year Round* office he proved to have none of the literary skill that Dickens had suspected in him, and he decided to follow Walter to India and join the Bengal Mounted Police. While Frank was travelling to India, word reached his father that Walter had died suddenly in Calcutta of a blood-infection. He had left debts at his death. Dickens wrote not a word to Kate about their loss. Of the other sons, Sydney was doing well enough as a naval cadet, and Harry was shining in his school-work; but Alfred failed in his attempts at a military career, then a medical one, then a mercantile one, and at last went off to Australia. He was followed there, some time later, by the youngest son, Edward, a shy, awkward boy, for whom a change of schools had done little to improve what his father sadly recognized as a 'want of application'. Dickens complained, 'I expect to be presently presented with a smock frock, a pair of leather breeches, and a pewter watch, for having brought up the largest family ever known with the smallest disposition to do anything for themselves.'

Dickens's mother died in 1863, and he grieved for lost friends, for Augustus Egg, and Thackeray, who had been persuaded by Katey to reconcile their quarrel just a few days earlier: 'I love the man', Thackeray said, and shook hands with him. Dickens's own health was not good, with attacks of gout, facial neuralgia, and a degeneration of the heart.

Below left: The Chalet at Gad's Hill presented to Dickens by a French actor, Charles Fechter
Below right: Dickens's cat

219

Nothing would deflect him from his course of life, from toil at the magazine, exhaustion in leisure, and above all from the public readings. He craved the stimulus those audiences gave him, taking him out of himself, though he defended them on the grounds that he had so many mouths to feed. The income was certainly spectacular: a two-month tour of the provinces could net him a profit of some £3000, but sums in excess of £10,000 were mentioned if he would go to Australia or America. However he could now command a £1000 fee for a short story, and Chapman and Hall's advance on his next novel would be £6000, so the income was certainly not the only attraction of the readings.

In the autumn of 1861 he started a new three-month tour of England and Scotland. His manager, Arthur Smith, had died, and the new manager made mistake after mistake – no publicity, inaccurate publicity, lost tickets, overbooking – but Dickens was soon into his inimitable stride and recorded a series of triumphs. To his repertoire he had added scenes from *Nicholas Nickleby*, *David Copperfield* (to which the response was 'without precedent'), *A Tale of Two Cities*, and some of the Christmas stories he wrote every year for the magazine. At Newcastle a gas-light crashed down, and Dickens averted a dreadful panic by remaining calm, making a joke of it. 'The more you want of the master', one of the gas-engineers remarked afterwards, 'the more you'll find in him'. At Edinburgh, where far too

Right: Dickens caricatured as various characters from his novels

many people were admitted, Dickens allowed the overspill to crowd round his feet on the platform. When Prince Albert died, Dickens interrupted the tour in respect for the Queen, even though he found the national mourning extravagant, and the country (by the time of the Prince of Wales's wedding in 1863) 'be-princed to the last point of human endurance'. The provincial tour was followed, after only a month, by another series in London.

A year later there was a further London series stretching over three months. Carlyle went to one reading, and laughed so much that several times Dickens had to pause to give his old friend time to recover. 'Dickens does it capitally', the sceptical Carlyle reported, 'such as *it* is, acts better than any Macready in the world; a whole tragic comic heroic *theatre* visible, performing under one *hat*, and keeping us laughing – in a sorry sort of way some of us thought – the whole night.'

It was now Dickens's habit to rent a house in London for the spring, where he might visit Ellen two or three nights a week. He provided her with a cottage at Slough, then 'an establishment of her own' at Peckham, though gradually she became an accepted guest at Gad's Hill, too. Georgina was always affectionate to her. What Mary thought is not recorded, but Katey was her outspoken self, bitterly at first, then simply sad. 'She flattered him – he was ever appreciative of praise – and though she was not a good actress she had brains, which she used to educate herself, to bring her mind more on a level with his own. Who could blame her? He had the world at his feet. She was a young girl of eighteen, elated and proud to be noticed by him. I do not blame *her*. It is never one person's fault.' Her father was 'not a good man, but he was not a fast man ... he was wonderful.' His romance with Ellen, Katey added, was 'more tragic and far-reaching in its effect' than that of Nelson and Lady Hamilton. It is not the only hint that Ellen brought Dickens more misery than joy, and did not answer to that 'one happiness I have missed in life, one friend and companion I have never made', of which he had once complained to Forster.

What woman could? Years later, Ellen was said by a clergyman to have told him that she 'loathed the very thought of the intimacy'. Better evidence is that Dickens himself told a friend that it would be 'inexpressibly painful' to Ellen 'to think that you knew her history' – a history which, some have conjectured, may have included the birth of a child. The evidence glimpsed through layers of discretion suggests it was Dickens's will that forced the affair beyond the flirtation in which it started; and that Ellen's subsequent reaction against his desperate demand coloured the romance coldly. She was glad of his rich man's support, but resented the secrecy it entailed, in which shame bred. For his part, he was glad to love a young woman after many flirtatious fantasies, and the experience is reflected in the realistic young women of his last novels; but the secrecy bred guilt in him, and he can never have quite settled his conscience over his treatment of Kate. Whatever her faults, he had written affectionate and cheerful letters to her from Italy, five years before the break-up, which contradicts the impression he gave in his public statements that the marriage had been adrift for many years. On her deathbed, nine years after he died, Kate gave her daughter Katey all the letters her husband had ever sent her, asking that they be lodged at the British Museum, so that 'the world may know that he loved me once'.

It is likely that Ellen accompanied Dickens on some of his trips to France and Belgium. Paris he loved now for the high esteem in which it held not only himself but all men of letters. He gave three readings at the British Embassy there in January 1863, and reported 'Blazes of Triumph.... They are so extraordinarily quick to understand a face and gesture ... that people who don't understand English, positively understand the Readings! I suppose that such an audience for a piece of Art is not to be found in the world.'

Ellen was certainly with him in Paris in the spring of 1865, for she was involved with him in a terrible railway accident in Kent, on their way home. The line was being repaired near Staplehurst. The driver was not given the proper signal, and the engine crashed through a bridge into a river, dragging the first coach with it. The second, in which Dickens and Ellen were travelling, halted on the brink, its rear end slewing down into a field. The coaches behind them went sideways

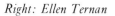

Right: Ellen Ternan

over the embankment and smashed on the ground.

Thrown into a corner, Dickens instantly calmed Ellen and an old lady in the compartment with them. 'We can't help ourselves', he said, 'but we can be quiet and composed. Pray don't cry out.' The old lady answered, 'Thank you. Rely on me. Upon my soul I will be quiet.' Dickens climbed out through a window, and saw a scene of panic and horror. He obtained a key to open the door and released all the passengers in their coach. Then with a flask of brandy and his hat filled with water he went among the injured and dying, giving what aid he could.

Back in London, he wrote to the railway asking about some trinkets that a lady had lost in the accident, including 'a gold seal engraved "Ellen"'. He was shaken, he said, 'not by the beating of the carriage, but by the work afterwards of getting out the dying and the dead'. It took him a long time to get over the shock, and he never lost 'sudden vague rushes of terror' when travelling. While still recovering, he was concerned for Ellen, telling one of his servants, 'Take Miss Ellen tomorrow morning, a little basket of fresh fruit, a jar of clotted cream from Tuckers, and a chicken, a pair of pigeons, or some nice little bird. Also on Wednesday morning, and on Friday morning, take her some other things of the same sort – making a little variety each day.'

Left: The Staplehurst railway accident, 9 June 1865

Above: 'The Happy Pair' by Marcus Stone for Our Mutual Friend

One thing he had remembered to retrieve from the crash was the manuscript of the latest instalment of the new book he was now writing in monthly parts, *Our Mutual Friend*. 'All this unsettled fluctuating distress in my mind' had caused a gap of three years since the completion of *Great Expectations*, but in the spring of 1864 he had got the new story started, and it was soon selling thirty thousand copies. A touching letter has survived in which Kate asks Chapman to send her the monthly instalments.

The book, the only one strictly contemporary in its setting, was Dickens's last and bitterest assault on the vulgar smugness of the bourgeoisie, which he now identified as the rotten core of everything he hated in the country. Their triumphant greed, their revaluation of human kind in cash, is symbolically rooted in the great heaps of dust and dung which surround London – 'a hopeless city, with no rent in the leaden canopy of its sky' – and supply scavenged wealth. Intensifying his savage attack, by contrast, is the most realistic picture he drew of the pain in love, the supreme human redemption.

Dickens's own experience can be traced easily enough in such a theme. The argument can also be equated, as it has been, with his belief in the New Testament and his despair, at this time, with the obfuscation of the church in England, still opposing science with Old Testament superstitions. 'The Church's hand is at its own throat.'

Chapter Twenty-five

Nearly Used Up

THE TITLE OF *All The Year Round* APTLY DESCRIBED THE assiduity with which Dickens edited it and its predecessor. From Paris, for instance, during an extended stay there, he wrote to Wilkie Collins, who was ill, offering to help him keep up the weekly schedule of a story, if Collins wished, by undertaking to 'ghost' it himself. 'I am quite confident that, with your notes and a few words of explanation, I could take it up at any time, and do it. Absurdly unnecessary to say that it would be a makeshift! But I could do it, at a pinch, so like you as that no one should find out the difference.'

However, after he had completed *Our Mutual Friend* Dickens's energies were directed, most of the time, into further series of readings. From the spring of 1866 the London firm of Chappell's were his promoters, paying him, at first, £50 a night plus expenses. They handled all the arrangements, and appointed a manager, George Dolby, a large, bald, amiable man, whom Dickens found to be 'an agreeable companion, an excellent manager, and a good fellow'. Dickens insisted that some good seats should continue to be available at a shilling each: 'I have been the champion and friend of the working man all through my career, and it would be inconsistent, if not unjust, to put any difficulty in the way of his attending my Readings.'

Starting in London, the first tour for Chappell's ranged up to Aberdeen and down to Portsmouth, drawing capacity audiences. Wills accompanied Dickens and Dolby, and the three passed the long train journeys eating from a hamper, drinking punch cooled in a wash-basin, singing, and playing cards and games; once Dickens did a hornpipe, while his companions whistled the tune. He was troubled by various ailments and slept poorly. To keep up his spirits at the interval of a reading, he would wash down a dozen of oysters with champagne. In Portsmouth, near the end of the tour, he visited Landport Terrace, trying to choose the house where he was born. Close by, they wandered into a redbrick square which irresistibly reminded Dickens of a pantomime set. He did his 'Grimaldi' for his companions, knocking on a door, lying down in front of it, feigning sleep. He was chased off by a fat, cross woman, losing his hat in the wind.

Six months later he was off again, undertaking, for £2500, to give forty-two performances, including some in Ireland during the Fenian troubles. By now he had a travelling valet called Scott, and between them Dolby and Scott made everything 'as easy to me as it possibly *can* be'. But Dickens still suffered from the strain, lying awake at nights and needing to rest on a sofa after his performance.

At Birmingham there was another incident with a gas-lamp, which he handled coolly again. A hanging-wire was burning through and the lamp threatened the front stalls. While Dickens was still reading, Dolby, behind a screen, whispered, 'How long shall you be?' 'Not long', Dickens indicated, without pausing. He improvised a rapid conclusion so adroitly that no-one guessed what he was doing. Afterwards he told Dolby he had noticed the danger long before the end, calculated how long he had got, and paced himself in accordance.

By the end of the tour, in May, Dickens was utterly exhausted. He was cast down, also, by the death of Stanfield, at whose deathbed he had, at the dying man's request, been reconciled with Mark Lemon – Lemon, who had sat with Dickens through the vigil over his own dead Dora sixteen years before. Yet now Dickens 'began to feel myself drawn towards America'. It was not the first time he had thought of readings in that country, but it had been ruled out for some years by the Civil War (a war which had little to do with slavery, in his opinion). He had considered Australia as an alternative: it would be 'a penance and a misery', for 'the domestic life of the Readings is all but intolerable to me when I am away for a few weeks at a time merely'; 'how painfully unwilling I am to go', he told Forster, 'and yet how painfully sensible that perhaps I ought to go – with all the hands upon my skirts that I cannot fail to feel and see there, whenever I look round.'

Now the war in America was over, and he was being offered guarantees of at least £10,000 to travel there. But how could he leave all those he loved? He exclaimed to Forster, 'I should be wretched beyond expression there. My small powers of description cannot describe the state of mind in which I should drag on from day to day.' Forster agreed. So did Wills. His health would not stand up. Even as a young man, he had been drained by that country. Besides, the recent war had sapped the American economy, and it could not be a profitable tour. So it was decided that he would go. The will of steel commanded the fatigue of his body. Anyway, in England he would not rest.

Dolby was sent to sniff out the trail. He came back enthusiastic. The Americans were all for it. Dickens belonged to them even more than to his own country, they said; a few thought a preliminary apology for what he had written a quarter of a century ago might be in order, but the majority believed that those sensitive memories had been covered over by history. The accommodations were already booked. The profit could exceed £15,000. It was announced: Dickens would arrive in Boston on 19 November 1867.

The old scars did ache, briefly, when the American press heard he was coming, but Dickens soothed them. Only once in twenty years, he said, had he referred to international copyright, and then it was in good-humoured complaint that, with such a law, 'I should have been a man of very large fortune, instead of a man of moderate savings.' It had, in fact, become customary for him to receive £1000

Below: George Dolby, 'an agreeable companion, an excellent manager and a good fellow'

Right: One of a series of photographs taken by Gurney during Dickens's second trip to America in 1867

from an American publisher in return for advance proof-sheets of his books.

Few celebrities were missing at the decorated feast given to bid him farewell. There were speeches, cheers, napkins and fans waved in the air, the band of the Grenadier Guards, and tears trickling down the cheeks of the guest of honour. Kate wrote to wish him well. He wrote back, 'I am glad to receive your letter, and to accept and reciprocate your good wishes. Severely hard work lies before me; but that is not a new thing in my life, and I am content to go my way and do it.'

Ellen was on his mind, of course. Wills was to look after her needs, but might there not be just a possibility that, with discretion, she could join him over there? A telegram code was arranged.

No sooner had he arrived in Boston (after another encounter between the ship and a mudbank) than he knew it would not be possible. As he ate his supper he saw eyes peering through the crack of the door at him: 'these people', he declared, 'have not in the least changed'. The word went round Boston that Mr Dickens did not wish to be mobbed, glad-handed or put on display, and he was treated respectfully as he walked round the city, *en fête* for his presence, but the eyes never left him; the people had changed, but not enough, and the coded telegram sadly renounced his hope of greeting Ellen.

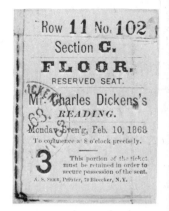

Above: An admission ticket to a reading in New York

He had a fortnight's rest before the first readings, and met Longfellow, Emerson, Putnam and other old friends. Meanwhile people were queuing overnight to buy seats and, if unlucky, paying touts ten times or more the price of a ticket. When they heard him, they decided it was worth every cent. 'Raptures' and 'star-shower' will stand for the garland of praise and applause. It was the same in New York, riots for tickets, ecstasies of applause, and in Philadelphia, and Baltimore. In Washington, President Andrew Johnson and the whole establishment politely clapped him, and on his birthday flowers were sent that filled his room. Everywhere he went there were flowers, too, from Mary Boyle, who somehow contrived to keep up her custom of supplying his buttonhole.

The press was fanciful but courteous, with the exception of the papers in Chicago which, when Dickens decided that he could not go West, rose up with accusations that he was ashamed to face the woman and children who had been left there by his late brother Augustus. Dickens disdained to reply that he had been in the habit of sending £50 a year to those people, no legal relations of his; he might as well have asserted that he was giving money to Edgar Allan Poe's mother-in-law, which was also true. At the same time he was writing to Mary to provide for Anne, their servant, who had first joined the family for the previous American journey, and he was paying for *The Old Curiosity Shop* to be printed in Braille for the blind people of Boston.

Already he was losing the gamble on his health. The 'true American catarrh' had gripped him, and would not be shifted, in the overheated rooms and railway carriages. With it, his heart trouble recurred and his difficulty in sleeping. After reading on Christmas night he 'was laid on a bed, in a very faint and shady state'; the doctors told him to rest for some days, but the next night he forced himself onto the platform again. Once he was up there, he always found a reserve of strength: 'the frequent experience of this return of force when it is wanted saves me a vast amount of anxiety, but I am not at times without the nervous dread that I may some day sink altogether.'

He arrived back in Boston on the day that President Johnson was impeached, and the event for once drew the attention from Dickens, so that a few readings were cancelled. The rest did him some good, and his high spirits surfaced. Clowning, elegant in evening dress, on the edge of a bathtub, in he goes, splash, not like Grimaldi. At a dinner party, burlesquing the British hustings, Dickens is the agent for the candidate Dolby, whose claim on the voters is that very few hairs corrupt his pate, and after Dickens has fetched everybody to 'agonies of laughter ... we roared and writhed' (said one), he is a multitude heckling at the rival agent. By children he is remembered in diaries as the kind, attentive, funny man, who sometimes had tears in his eyes.

And on again, through snow and flood in New England, and the

true American ... came back as bad as ever. I have coughed from two or three in the morning until five or six, and have been absolutely sleepless. I have had no appetite besides, and no taste. Last night I took some laudanum, and it is the only thing that has done me good.... I am nearly used up. Climate, distance, catarrh, travelling, and hard work have begun (I may say so, now they are nearly over) to tell heavily upon me.

The 'low action of the heart' was aggravated by the excitement and energy of the performances, so that his hands were black with blood, his face changing hues. Dolby, 'tender as a woman', and Doctor Fordyce Barker watched him through each day. His diet: 'At seven in the morning, in bed, a tumbler of cream and two tablespoonsful of rum. At twelve, a sherry cobbler and a biscuit. At three (dinner time), a pint of champagne. At five minutes to eight, an egg beaten up with a glass of sherry. Between the parts, the strongest beef tea that can be made, drunk hot. At a quarter past ten, soup, and anything to drink that I can fancy.' The gout, which in England had grown so painful that sometimes he could not put a shoe on, now lamed him again, so that he staggered into a New York press banquet on the arm of Horace Greeley.

He spoke there of

the national generosity and magnanimity ... amazing changes I have seen around me.... Nor am I, believe me, so arrogant as to suppose that in twenty-five years there have been no changes in me, and that I had nothing to learn and no extreme impressions to correct when I was here first.... I have been received with unsurpassable politeness, delicacy, sweet temper, hospitality, consideration, and with unsurpassable respect for the privacy daily enforced upon me by the nature of my avocation here, and the state of my health. This testimony, so long as I live, and so long as my descendants have any legal right in my books I shall cause to be republished as an appendix to those two books of mine in which I have referred to America.

Five months after arriving, he gave his seventy-sixth reading of the tour, and two days later pelted by flowers he steamed out of New York. To a proposal that a statue should be erected in honour of his heroism, he answered, 'No, don't; take down one of the old ones instead!'

Chapter Twenty-six

Half Made Up of Partings

ALONG THE ROAD TO GAD'S HILL THERE WERE FLAGS BEDECKING the houses and shouts of 'Welcome home, sir.' The voyage had restored his health, and he could walk again. Soon he was greeting friends who followed him from America, including Longfellow and Doctor Fordyce Barker, running them round in a coach with postillions dressed 'in the old red jacket of the old red royal Dover road', and leading them (with police protection) through the low life and opium dens of the dockside. A Christmas story, *No Thoroughfare*, on which he had collaborated with Collins, was staged in London, with Fechter in the lead: Dickens improved the production, then visited Paris to assist with a French production of the same piece.

His other commitments included an increased burden of management at *All The Year Round*, since Wills had been forced to retire after a hunting accident. Charley, whose business had gone bankrupt, was taken on as an assistant at the magazine, and to Dickens's pleasure proved so apt at the work that eventually he was bequeathed his father's three-quarter share.

Harry, always the most promising of Dickens's sons, won a mathematics scholarship at Cambridge. Dickens, when he heard the news, nodded, 'Capital! Capital!' and was sunk in reflection. On what – the contrast with his six other sons? – with his own youthful dream of being 'distinguished at a grammar-school, and going to Cambridge'? Harry was 'somewhat disappointed' by his father's restraint as they walked home. Then Dickens took his son's hand and, tears in his eyes, muttered 'God bless you, my boy.'

Much less satisfactory was the development of Sydney, the naval cadet. He fell into debt and showed no sign of mending. Dickens, deeply disappointed, told him that he would not be welcome at Gad's Hill.

Edward had left for Australia, though the news soon came back that he was unsettled there. At their parting, 'he seemed to me to become once more my youngest and favourite child', Dickens wrote, 'and I did not think I could have been so shaken.' In his farewell letter to the boy, he wrote,

I love you dearly, and am very, very sorry in my heart to part with you. But this life is half made up of partings. . . . Never take a mean advantage of anyone in any transaction, and never be hard upon people who are in your power. . . . As your brothers have gone away, one by one, I have written to each such words as I am now writing to you. . . . I hope you will always be able to say in after life, that you had a kind father.

It was more than a piety. Dickens was anxious about what he had been to his children, and what he had done for his sons. Edward, his darling little 'Plorn', was not keen to go to Australia. Dickens's grief was genuine, but it was self-inflicted. Like his six brothers, Edward was told by his father, 'I was not so old as you are now when I first had to win my food.' Dickens, for whom education was the pass-key to all social problems, halted his own sons' education (and his brother Fred's) the moment they were 'manly' enough to make their own way in life. The sole exception, Harry, was something of a mystery to his father, who understood little of universities, the higher teaching, stimulating the life of the mind – his own mind, after all, Dickens knew to have the richest imaginable life, and it had not been trained at a university. Primary education was a different matter, a practical necessity until the age of self-reliance. Then – moved by the insecurity of his own childhood, and his confirmed fears that 'want of application' ran in the family – Dickens sent his sons off to make their own, honest, hard-working way, and for most of them that meant travelling half-way round the world, to the imperial opportunities. But – again, ironically, with the exception of Harry, who became a knighted lawyer – it did not work. For all the 'kindness' Dickens hoped he had shown, he was so exacting that they, like their mother, could not live up to his standards, nor prosper in the shadow of his own gigantic success.

Outside his fiction, that steel will, forged in youth, could be as authoritarian in private matters as it was in dealing with publishers. Though he despised lawyers and parliamentarians, and to the end of his life believed that 'law-givers are nearly always the obstructors of society, instead of its helpers', he was capable of prosecuting a poor Irish girl for shouting abuse in the public street. He deplored the slums in which crime was bred, but had scant sympathy for criminals; just as he deplored the injustices which fanned revolution, but was at the least ambiguous in his attitude to the mobs, destroying property or reappropriating it, that revolution engenders. The least abstract of writers, he tended to rigid, theoretical behaviour in private, rising hysterically when baulked, by publishers, by friends, by Kate, by his own invalid body. With his family there was also, as he acknowledged, that old 'habit of suppression', so clear in his reaction to Harry's news from Cambridge.

Dickens's brother Fred died, and the harrowing toll went on among friends: Maclise, soon followed by Lemon. Yet Dickens was willing, indeed eager, to risk his own health more rashly than ever. Even before his return from America, with a profit of £20,000, he had contracted with Chappell's to give another hundred readings in Britain, for £8000. It would, he promised, be his farewell tour.

He was embracing death. Already the invigoration of the Atlantic had been sapped. He was tired, sleepless, bilious, and afflicted with occasional weakness of sight on one side.

Overleaf: 'Dickens's Dream' by R. W. Buss

MR. CHARLES DICKENS'S
𝔉𝔞𝔯𝔢𝔴𝔢𝔩𝔩 ℜ𝔢𝔞𝔡𝔦𝔫𝔤𝔰.

Mr. CHARLES DICKENS has resumed his Series of Farewell Readings at

ST. JAMES'S HALL, PICCADILLY.

The Readings will take place as follows:

TUESDAY EVENING, FEBRUARY 8, The Story of Little Dombey (last time) and Mr. Bob Sawyer's Party (from Pickwick).

TUESDAY EVENING, FEBRUARY 15, Boots at the Holly Tree Inn; Sikes and Nancy (from Oliver Twist); and Mrs. Gamp (last time).

TUESDAY EVENING, FEBRUARY 22, Nicholas Nickleby (at Mr. Squeers's School, last time); and Mr. Chops, the Dwarf (last time).

TUESDAY EVENING, MARCH 1, David Copperfield (last time), and The Trial from Pickwick.

TUESDAY EVENING, MARCH 8, Boots at the Holly Tree Inn (last time); Sikes and Nancy (from Oliver Twist, last time); and Mr. Bob Sawyer's Party (from Pickwick, last time).

TUESDAY EVENING, MARCH 15, FINAL FAREWELL READING, The Christmas Carol (last time), and The Trial from Pickwick (last time).

To commence each Evening at Eight o'Clock.

No Readings will take place out of London.

PRICES OF ADMISSION:

SOFA STALLS, 7s.; STALLS, 5s.; BALCONY, 3s.;
Admission—ONE SHILLING.

Tickets may be obtained at CHAPPELL & Co.'s, 50, New Bond Street.

The readings began in October 1868, but shortly Dickens wanted to introduce a new scene. Charley was the first audience. He was sitting in Gad's Hill Place when he heard bellowing and screaming in the garden. He ran out. In the meadow, his father was Bill Sikes murdering Nancy, fleeing, dying. Charley, asked for his opinion, said, 'The finest thing I have ever heard, but don't do it.' He knew it would murder his father. Dickens, however, was worried about the audience: it would 'petrify' them all right, but it might frighten them away. Forster's view was the same as Charley's; so was Dolby's and Edmund Yates's. Dickens decided to put it to the test of an invited audience of friends. Beforehand, a doctor warned him it could produce mass hysteria. Afterwards a clergyman confirmed 'an almost irresistible impulse upon me to *scream*'. An actress admired the performance: 'Having got at such an effect as that, it must be done.' What did Charley think now? 'It is finer even than I expected, but I still say, don't do it.' Dickens did not understand. Charley would not give his reason, knowing it would merely irritate his father. In January 1869, after some more readings in the provinces, the Murder was performed in London. Dickens lay in bed the next morning, still exhausted.

The final appearances in Ireland followed. Dickens, accompanied by Mary and Georgina, was in another train accident, when a driving-wheel exploded and hurled shrapnel along the carriages. They shuddered to a halt. No one was seriously injured, but the incident served to re-ignite Dickens's fears of travelling, never extinguished since Staplehurst.

He was including the Murder in most of his programmes now. Ladies fainted in dozens, but the breathless admiration of professional actresses encouraged him to persevere in spite of the cost to his body. He went lame again, and was forbidden by a doctor to go on. He observed the advice for a few days, then travelled to Edinburgh, where he was again unable to stand until a doctor prescribed a special boot. By now everyone close to him wanted him to stop the readings. Not until he had completed the series of a hundred, he answered, then he supposed he would be glad to have done with it. 'Anyhow, I think so *now*.' It is doubtful if he did think so, at any time. The Murder was a new and particular joy, arousing 'a fixed expression of horror of me, all over the theatre, which could not have been surpassed if I had been going to be hanged'. From his last reading in Edinburgh he lurched to the sofa in his dressing-room unable to speak. Dolby told him it was unnecessarily lacerating him to do the Murder so often, when other readings would be quite as gladly received. 'Have you finished?' Dickens shouted. He hurled down his knife and fork, breaking a plate in pieces. 'Dolby! your infernal caution will be your ruin.' Dolby turned away from the first anger he had seen in the man. 'Forgive me, Dolby.' Dickens, weeping now, embraced his manager. 'I really didn't mean it; and I know you are right.' In his eyes, Dolby used to say, 'lurked the iron will of a demon and the tender pity of an angel'.

He was bleeding internally some days, limping, giddy, and always exhausted. His 'weakness and deadness' were, he said, 'all *on the left side*, and if I don't look at anything I try to touch with my hand, I don't know where it is'. One doctor, then another, diagnosed incipient paralysis and the risk of a stroke. The readings had to stop. Very well, although there were twenty-six readings still to do, he would stop: or rather, rest for some months, and then resume. 'My poor boy', Dickens sobbed to Dolby, 'I am so sorry for all the trouble I am giving you.'

Resting, he was not content merely to edit and manage the magazine. It was time to think of a new book. Chapman and Hall advanced £7500 on a contract in which Dickens had inserted a clause directing that a proportion of the advance be repaid if he were prevented from completing the book by death or permanent disablement. When he started to write *The Mystery of Edwin Drood*, he wove together the themes of death and murder, the pain of loving and a shadowed soul. It is a mystery in the sinister sense – who killed whom? – but also in the more profound sense, where (as in a short story written not long previously) the questions prowl around the ambiguity of a man's personality, the faces he turns to the world.

At this time Dickens made his will. His first bequest is inexplicable: £1000 to Ellen Ternan. It was not enough to provide for her permanently, but sufficient to advise the posthumous world of what had been so discreetly veiled while he lived. Georgina was left £8000, most of his jewellery, his private papers, and the enjoined gratitude of his children for all that she had been to them. To Kate he assured a continuing small income while she lived; since their separation, the will records, 'all the great charges of a numerous and expensive family have devolved wholly upon myself'. Charley inherited the library. Excepting a few small gifts to friends and servants, the rest was divided among the children. The total estate, at his death, would prove to be £93,000, some half of which was attributable to the readings.

Another twelve were arranged, to be performed in London between January and March 1870. The prospect kept Dickens's spirits up as he worked in the chalet at Gad's Hill on the early instalments of *Edwin Drood*, and strolled in the afternoon round the Medway countryside. The hand and foot on his left side still gave him some trouble, but he was not anxious enough to consider dropping the Murder from his programme. At every reading there would be a doctor, who himself arranged that Charley would always be there, too, 'and if you see your father falter in the least, you must run and catch him and bring him off to me, or, by Heaven, he'll die before them all.'

The opening night, with no Murder, went well, but Dickens's pulse was found to have risen from 72 to 95. Now the mere anticipation of performing Bill Sikes raised his pulse to 90, and after the reading it was 112. As the performances went on, his excitement continued to mount, and so did his pulse, reaching 124. At the

Opposite: 'Opium Smoking – The Lascar's Room in Edwin Drood' *depicted by G. Doré*

intervals he was half-carried to a sofa, where he lay without breath to speak until he was revived with brandy. After the readings, he was prostrated. His hand swelled up and had to be carried in a sling. By the last reading, his power of speech was weakening. He repeatedly mispronounced 'Pickwick' in the trial scene from that book. When it was done, over two thousand people in St James's Hall rose to him. He had to return to the platform, where he faced the ovation, tears wetting his cheeks. 'From these garish lights', he said, 'I now vanish for ever more, with a heartfelt, grateful, respectful, affectionate farewell.' He left, was recalled again, kissed his hand to the audience, and then it was finished.

A few days later the Queen, at a private audience, regretted that she had not heard a reading. Dickens was unable to offer to give a private one for her, not on the grounds of infirmity, but because, he told her, a mixed-class audience was essential to him. Etiquette kept him on his feet for the ninety minutes of their conversation; respect kept Victoria on hers.

When the first monthly number of *Edwin Drood* was published, its sales 'very, very far outstripped every one of its predecessors'. While he continued to work at the book and the magazine, he spent the spring in London in a round of dinners, speeches, a breakfast with the Prime Minister, Gladstone, a visit to the theatre where, according to Lord Redesdale, he sparkled like champagne. But 'the old convivial gatherings with equals were gone for ever', Una Pope-Hennessy remarks. 'He now had to make do with celebrities.' There was one more onset of Thespianism, when, though prevented by lameness from acting, he rehearsed and stage-managed everything. He could never have been a great dramatist, for the controlling narrative voice was indispensable to his imagination. But it was a 'cherished day-dream' of his, he remarked, to be the director of a 'skilled and noble' theatre company.

He was yearning for Kent again, 'weary of this London dining-out'. He would return as soon as the play was over. On his last afternoon at the magazine office there were tears in his eyes when it was time to say farewell to Dolby. He stood to shake hands, looked into his manager's eyes, and said, 'Goodbye, Dolby, old man.'

Chapter Twenty-seven

The Journey is Worked Out

IT WAS DELIGHTFUL TO BE BACK IN THE JUNE COUNTRYSIDE, to be able, after supper on the Sunday, to sit on at the table listening to Mary singing in the drawing-room, and to talk to Katey until dawn, the sweet night air fanning them through open windows. Katey had an idea of going on the stage; he dissuaded her (she eventually had some success as an artist), and then 'talked and talked' as she had never heard him before. He wished, he told her, that he had been 'a better father, and a better man'.

A few hours later, Katey was waiting for the carriage to take her to the station. She had to spend the week in London. Her father did not like to say goodbyes, and anyway he was already up and writing in the chalet, and it would be better not to interrupt him. She left a message of farewell. But as she waited, her mind changed. She went into the chalet, and up to his room among the tree-tops. Instead of absent-mindedly offering his cheek, he kissed her affectionately. How worn and grey his face looked. On her way back through the tunnel, she was impelled to return to him. 'He pushed his chair back from the writing table, opened his arms, and took me into them.' As she travelled to London, she found herself saying, 'I am so glad I went – I am so glad.'

Right: A caricature by Spy (Leslie Ward) in 1870

Mary followed Katey to London the next day. On Wednesday, 8 June Dickens abandoned his habit of walking in the afternoon, and instead worked at his book in the chalet. In the evening he wrote some letters, quoting, in one of them, Friar Laurence's warning to Romeo: 'These violent delights have violent ends.'

At supper, Georgina saw he was ill. Yes, he said, he had been very ill for an hour past. No, he did not want to call a doctor. He wished the meal to continue. He muttered a few remarks to himself, something about toothache, then declared that he must at once leave for London. He stood up, and Georgina rushed round the table to catch his falling body. He was too heavy for her to carry him to the sofa. She laid him down on the floor and heard him murmur, 'On the ground.'

Servants lifted him to the sofa, while Georgina sent word to the family. Doctors were fetched, saw that he had had a stroke, and preferred to let him remain where he was, on the sofa, all night and the next day. Charley arrived, so did Mary and Katey, Ellen Ternan and Mary Boyle. Dickens lay unconscious, breathing heavily, until the early evening. Then he sighed, a tear trickled between closed eyelids, and he died.

Above: Georgina Hogarth in old age

The last page he had written, in *Edwin Drood*, was a description of Rochester, the place where his first novel *Pickwick* began. He wrote it only a few miles away from Rochester, amid the countryside in which he had spent the years of his life when 'everything was happy, when there was no distance and no time'. Rochester, Chatham and Lucy Stroughill all seemed withered when he revisited them as a man. But 'who was I to quarrel with the town for having changed to me, when I myself had come back, so changed . . . so much the wiser and so much the worse?'

The pain of knowing: that is the original meaning of the word 'nostalgia'. If the sentimentality can be scrubbed from it, the word will serve as a key to Dickens's life, and take us far into his work. His astounding, restless energy, his magnificent achievement, and the disappointment in which he died, all sprang from the pain of knowing, the 'vague unhappy loss or want of something'. The sense of loss could be attached to particular losses in his adult life, which were always lost ideals, whether it be the vision of Mary Hogarth or the vision of republican America; but it is impossible not to refer them all back to the original loss, of innocence (and perhaps further back still, as in *David Copperfield*, to the loss of the seraphic mother). The buoyant gusto and brave spirits that his friends enjoyed in his life and we enjoy in his books are the best humours of childhood: as they are increasingly shadowed by greed, suffering, evil, what moves us is the intuition that things could be otherwise, because, in the little society of a family, they once were otherwise. As Dickens put it, his memory of childhood was 'the best and purest link between this world and a better', and he 'did not care to resist' its attraction. His delight in experience, in the peculiarity of character and place, is the delight that innocence takes before it has been taught to stand back, categorize, abstract, rationalize. The exaggeration of his caricatures is the

Below: Dickens on his deathbed by Sir John Everett Millais

exaggeration of a child faced with novel, formed characters every day. Of no one can it be more truly said than of Dickens that the child was father of the man. That is why his life reads like a novel.

The world of his childhood is vital in another sense to the understanding of his work. It was as a child that he heard, around him, the speech of people born and bred in the eighteenth century, and he immersed himself in the classic novels of English literature, which deeply influenced him as a writer, especially in his earlier works. It is not just a question of picaresque constructions, but of the very tone of voice he adopts: the 'mock verbosity', in Angus Wilson's phrase, revelling in parody, irony, hyperbole. Writing at the intersection of the Romantic-Regency epoch and the full-blown industrialism of the Victorian era, he brought to what

are still, in essence, modern problems the language of an earlier way of life in England. Like all the classic humorists, he was on the side of sanity against excess; and like them he fought excess with greater excess.

Of course he developed. His earlier novels, as J.B. Priestley points out, 'are never strictly contemporary but appear to be set back in time, somewhere around 1820, especially in their happier passages'. The great books of his maturity leave the decade of his childhood behind and enter the period which was father to our own. At the same time, his sense that men of goodwill could solve the abuses of society altered – in his novels, if not in his journalism and public statements – into a despair of ever blowing away the fog and dismantling 'the system'. But the despair always expressed itself in image, metaphor, absurdity, symbol so shining that, like gold, it glows today as brightly as it did then. He was the first great writer to confront the social problems he saw around him, and he remains the poet of the politico-economic wasteland we still, unhappily, inhabit, even though the abuses are not as vividly before our eyes as they were in Dickens's time. He, with his vows to strike 'the heaviest blow in my power', 'a sledge-hammer blow', would not have refused the epithet 'a writer with a message'. On the contrary, he pointedly wrote about what his public could recognize, 'flattered its moral feelings' as Humphry House puts it. Like any good writer, he developed the habit of wasting nothing. His appeal has sounded to many millions of readers all round the globe, and even in his own time he was appreciated in countries far beyond his own. From the Crimean War he was sent bloodstained copies of his books translated into Russian. He has always been admired as a family entertainer, but to the poor his special message was that of a social champion.

As a world-famous and rich author he might have rested content when his body rebelled. But, he answered, 'I hold my inventive faculty on the stern condition that it must master my whole life, often have complete possession of me, make its own demands upon me and sometimes for months together put everything else away from me.' His son Charley was 'certain that the children of my father's brain were much more real to him at times than we were'. And so, 'driven by an irresistible might until the journey is worked out', his body finally lay dead, and the mystery of his life, like that of any man's life, was as unresolved as the half-written mystery across the Dover road.

He had wished for a quiet burial, in Rochester or a country churchyard. What he got was a grave in Westminster Abbey, demanded by *The Times* for the world's 'unassailable and enduring favourite', and seconded by the establishment of London. His family acquiesced, but insisted on the terms of the will: a private, un-advertised funeral, where no one should wear any 'scarf, cloak, black bow, long hatband, or other such revolting absurdity', and his name was to be engraved 'in plain English letters'. He had loathed the panoply of Wellington's obsequies.

While the burial was being prepared, Thomas Woolner took a death mask from

Below: The inscription on
Dickens's tombstone in
Poets' Corner, Westminster
Abbey

Dickens's face, and Millais sketched his head. Carlyle wrote to Forster that beneath Dickens's 'bright and joyful sympathy with everything around him' there had been, 'if one has the eye to see deep enough, dark, fateful silent elements, tragical to look upon, and hiding amid dazzling radiances as of the sun, the elements of death itself'. His passing was 'an event world-wide: a *unique* of talents suddenly extinct'.

The body was taken by a special train to Charing Cross. The mourners, among whom Kate was not numbered, followed the hearse to the Abbey in three carriages. The service was short, and ended with a dead march on the organ. Above the bell was tolling, and gradually London found out that Dickens was lying in Poets' Corner, in a grave that would be left open for a few days. The grave was closed by the flowers thrown in until they overflowed.

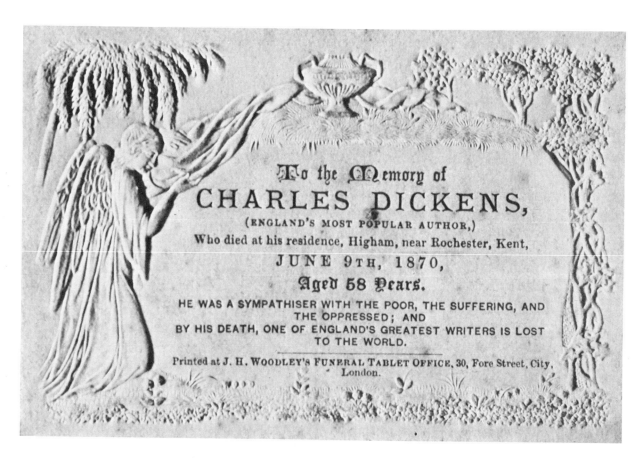

To the Memory of
CHARLES DICKENS,
(ENGLAND'S MOST POPULAR AUTHOR,)
Who died at his residence, Higham, near Rochester, Kent,
JUNE 9TH, 1870,
Aged 58 Years.
HE WAS A SYMPATHISER WITH THE POOR, THE SUFFERING, AND THE OPPRESSED; AND
BY HIS DEATH, ONE OF ENGLAND'S GREATEST WRITERS IS LOST TO THE WORLD.
Printed at J. H. WOODLEY'S FUNERAL TABLET OFFICE, 30, Fore Street, City, London.

Bibliography

Arthur A. Adrian, *Georgina Hogarth and the Dickens Circle* (London and New York, Oxford University Press, 1957)

Ivor Brown, *Dickens in his Time* (London, Thomas Nelson, 1963)

Ivor Brown, *Dickens and His World* (New York, H. Z. Walck, 1970)

John Butt and Kathleen Tillotson, *Dickens at Work* (London, Eyre Methuen, 1957; Fair Lawn, N. J., Essential Books, 1958)

Philip Collins (ed.), *Charles Dickens: The Public Readings* (London, Oxford University Press, 1976)

Walter Dexter, *The London of Dickens* (Palmer, 1930)

Henry Fielding Dickens, *Memories of My Father* (London, Heinemann, 1929; New York, Duffield & Co., 1929)

The Dickensian, quarterly journal (London, Dickens Fellowship)

The American Dickensian, quarterly journal (New York, The Dickens Fellowship, 1922–1930)

John Forster, *The Life of Charles Dickens*, ed. A. J. Hoppé (Philadelphia, J. B. Lippincott & Co., 1872–4) (London, Everyman's Library, Dent, 1966)

John Gross and Gabriel Pearson (eds), *Dickens and the Twentieth Century* (London, Routledge & Kegan Paul, 1962; Routledge paperback, 1966)

Christopher Hibbert, *The Making of Charles Dickens* (London, Longmans, 1967; New York, Harper & Row, 1967)

Humphrey House, *The Dickens World* (London, Oxford University Press, 1941; Oxford paperback, 1960)

Madeleine House and Graham Storey, *The Pilgrim Edition of the Letters of Charles Dickens*, 1820–39, 2 vols (Oxford, Clarendon Press, 1965)

Edgar Johnson, *Charles Dickens, his Tragedy and Triumph*, 2 vols (London, Victor Gollancz, 1953; New York, Simon and Schuster, 1952)

Jack Lindsay, *Dickens, a Biographical and Critical Study* (Dakers, 1950)

Sylvère Monod, *Dickens the Novelist*, trans. from French (Norman, University of Oklahoma Press, 1968)

Hesketh Pearson, *Dickens, his Character, Comedy and Career* (London, Eyre Methuen, 1949; New York, Harper, 1949)

Una Pope-Hennessy, Charles Dickens (London, Chatto & Windus, 1945; New York, Howell, Soskin, 1946)

J. B. Priestley, *Charles Dickens and his World* (London, Thames & Hudson, 1961)

Angus Wilson, *The World of Charles Dickens* (London, Secker & Warburg, 1970; Penguin paperback, 1972)

Acknowledgements

Photographs and illustrations are supplied by, or reproduced by kind permission of the following:

British Museum 70, *125 bottom*, 156, *192*;

Cooper-Bridgeman Library *37 bottom*, 92, *151*, *152*;

Courtesy of the Trustees of the Dickens House 8, 9, 11, 14, 16, 20 left, 20 right, 23, 29, 35, *37 top*, 42, 47, 48, 49 below left, 51, 55, 58, 65, 71, 79, 81 above, 91, 103, 105, 108, 110, 125 top, 126 top, 127, 133, 134, 139, 145 left, 146, 148, 161, 165, 168, 170, 182, *189*, 201, 210, 215, 219, left and right, 223, 224, 227, 234–5, 243, 244;

John Freeman and Co. 67, 113, 175;

Guildhall Library 18;

Harrogate Art Gallery *190–1*;

Mander and Mitchenson Collection 220, 228, 242;

Mansell Collection 30, 87, 120, 145 right, 179, 194 top and bottom, 209, 246;

Marylebone Public Library 88;

Museum of London *38–9*:

National Portrait Gallery 30, 49 right, 174;

Radio Times Hulton Picture Library 89, 97, 98, 99, 122, 124, 132, 157, 163, 172, 173, 181, 195, 203;

Royal Academy of Art *190–1*;

Royal Holloway College, Egham *37 bottom*;

Victoria and Albert Museum 12, *40*, 61, 68, 69, 74, 76, 81 left, 92, 94, 107, 113, 117, 118, *126 bottom*, 140, *151*, *152*, 154, 164, 187, *189*, 196, 222, 239;

Weidenfeld and Nicolson Archives 43, 88, 91, 170, 174, 175, 220, 236;

Emlyn Williams 62, 229,

Numbers in italics refer to colour illustrations.

Picture Research by Juliet Scott.

Index